YOUR BRAIN AND HOW IT WORKS

HERBERT S. ZIM

illustrated by René Martin

William Morrow and Company
New York 1972

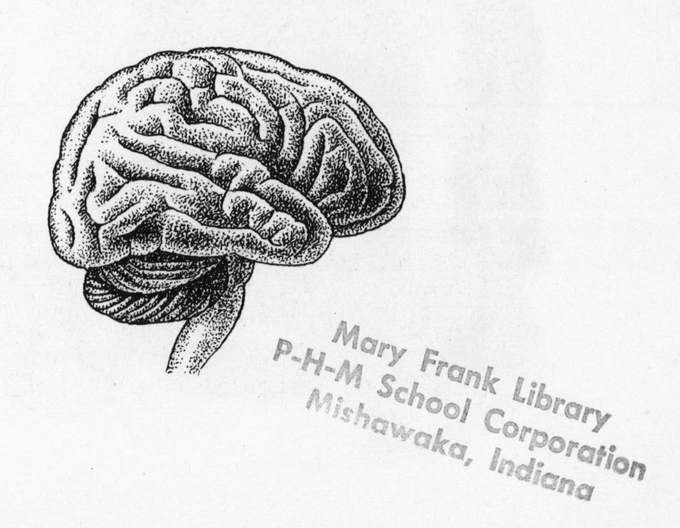

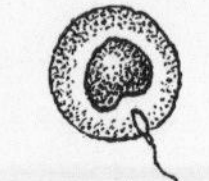

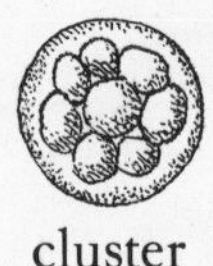
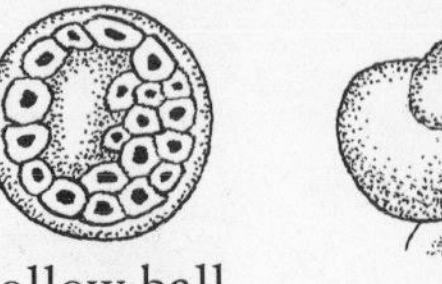

EARLY STAGES OF HUMAN EMBRYO

The author wishes to thank Daniel Bader and John A. Broward, neurologists, and Glenn V. Ross, physician, for their expert help in preparing this manuscript. This book is dedicated to Dr. Broward, who died on May 9, 1971.

A Rogewinn Book

Printed in the United States of America.

Library of Congress Catalog Card Number 78-168479

4 5

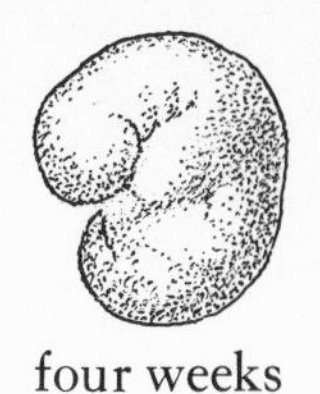

four weeks

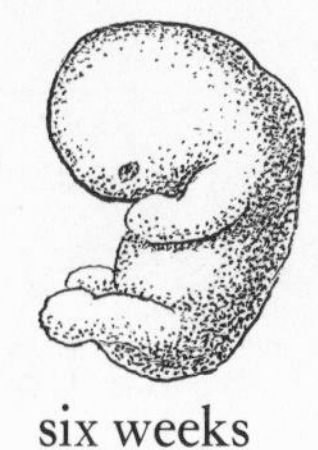

six weeks

actual length
one inch

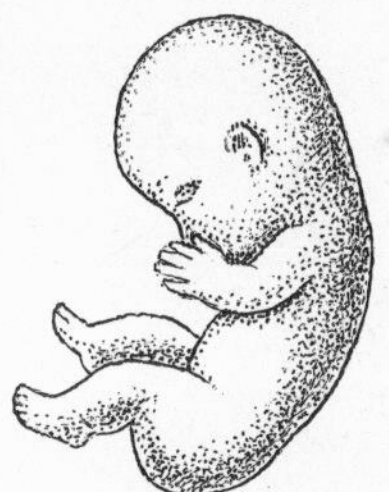

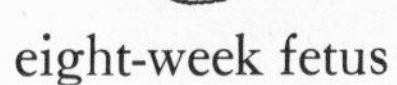

eight-week fetus

DEVELOPMENT OF BRAIN

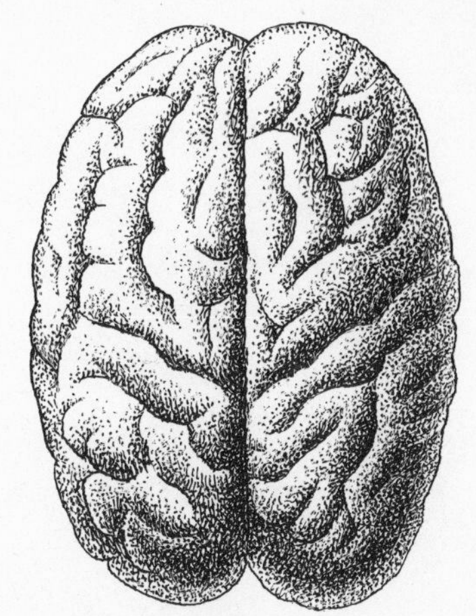

brain at birth

How does something as wonderful as your brain begin? The answer lies in the story of how you, yourself, began. As you well know, you first appeared as a single egg cell inside your mother, fertilized by a single sperm cell of your father. The cell grew, divided, again and again, first forming a ball. This ball filled out and gradually became a mass of cells about the size of a small bean.

By this time different kinds of cells were forming within the mass. One group of cells, made up from the outside layer, became the neural plate, the beginning of the nerves and the brain. The neural plate is a little wider at one end. This end is the beginning of the brain.

The neural plate folds in, forming a tube. As it grows, different types of nerve cells appear. At the wider end, cell growth produces a fold across the tube. Soon another fold forms close by. The front segment grows and swells the most, the middle one next. By the time an embryo has grown for a month, the three main parts of the brain have begun to take shape.

As the brain in an embryo grows the parts that receive smell and sight messages begin to develop first. Other distinct parts of the brain emerge. The front brain — or forebrain — unfolds, spreads, and covers some of the parts formed earlier. Canals develop, in which a fluid from the blood circulates, providing food and removing wastes from the brain cells. The brain itself is semisolid, not unlike gelatin or Jello.

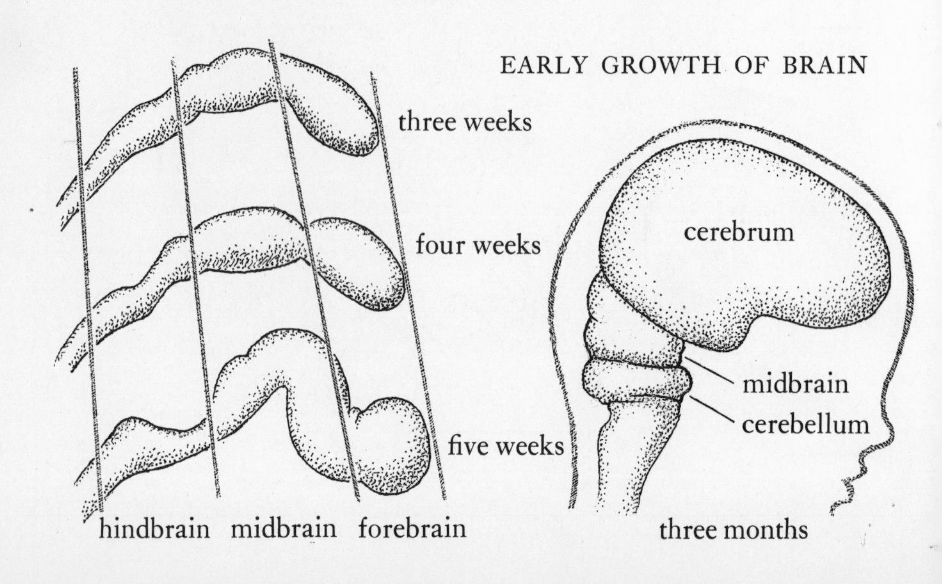

EARLY GROWTH OF BRAIN

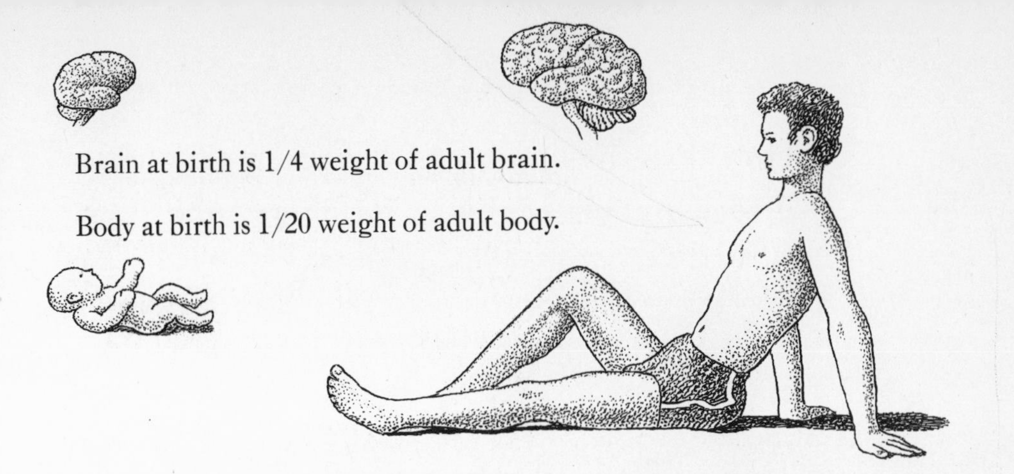

Well before birth all the brain cells you will ever have are formed. At birth the weight of a baby's brain is almost a pound, or about one seventh the weight of its body. No other animal has a brain as big in proportion to its body size when it is born. The weight of the newborn baby's brain is about 25 percent of its adult weight, although the weight of its body is only 5 percent of its adult weight. At six months a baby's brain is 50 percent of its adult weight, and at five years a child's brain is 90 percent. Some areas within the brain do not become mature till about age 35.

At birth most of the bones of the skull have formed, but the bones at the top of the skull have not yet joined. Their soft edges permit movement during birth and allow for the growth of the head and brain during early childhood.

How does the brain work? This simple question cannot be answered completely. The brain moves and controls muscles. It sends messages and stores information. But it does much more. It is involved in all the human activities we call our behavior. Some of these activities, like eating and breathing, keep us alive. Others, equally important, include all we do as we live, work, play, grow, and reproduce. Our behavior involves our curiosity and learning, our joys and sorrows, beliefs and ambitions. Often behavior includes and affects other people. In truth, our behavior makes us the individual human beings we are.

Everything we do is our behavior.

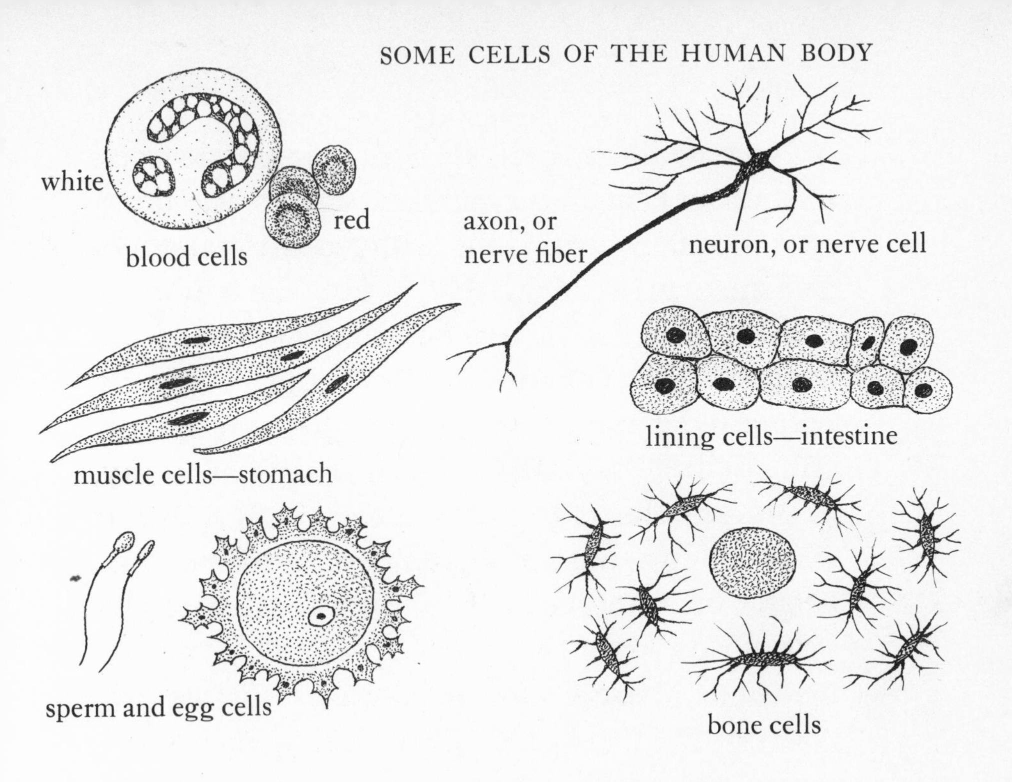

SOME CELLS OF THE HUMAN BODY

Your brain is only part of your system of nerves. It and the spinal cord make up your central nervous system. Both must be understood together. True, the brain is the most important part, but it is of no value without the spinal cord, the nerves, and most of your body. Your skull and backbone protect the brain and spinal cord. Your blood nourishes them. Billions of living cells form your bones, blood, muscles, and other tissues. Nerve cells, or neurons, are the units of your nervous system.

Nerve cells carry messages, and they do so by a complex chemical-electrical process. A critical place in the system is the synapse, the contact of one neuron with another. Here the outgoing branch of a neuron touches another's incoming branch. A new impulse starts and eventually reaches the brain. Many synapses are in the spinal cord, especially those that start an action to protect you in an emergency.

The long axons, or nerve fibers, of the neurons often form bundles. These bundles and their supporting cells are cell nerves. More than 75 percent of a nerve consists of cells that feed, insulate, and protect the nerve fibers, which in a large nerve may number thousands.

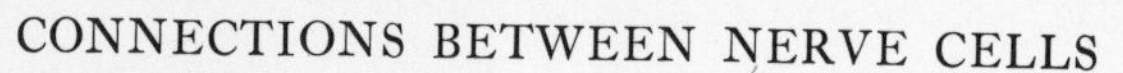

CONNECTIONS BETWEEN NERVE CELLS

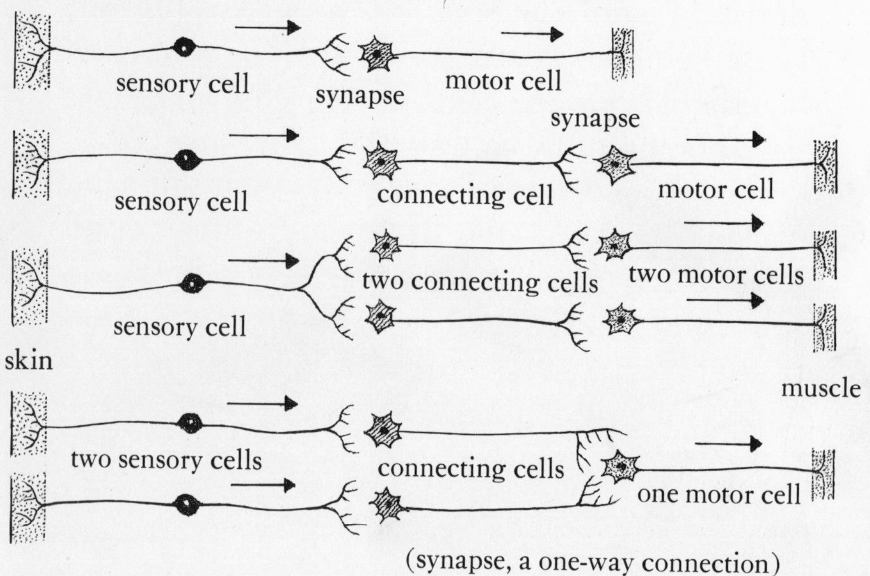

(synapse, a one-way connection)

STRUCTURE OF A NERVE FIBER (thinner than a hair)

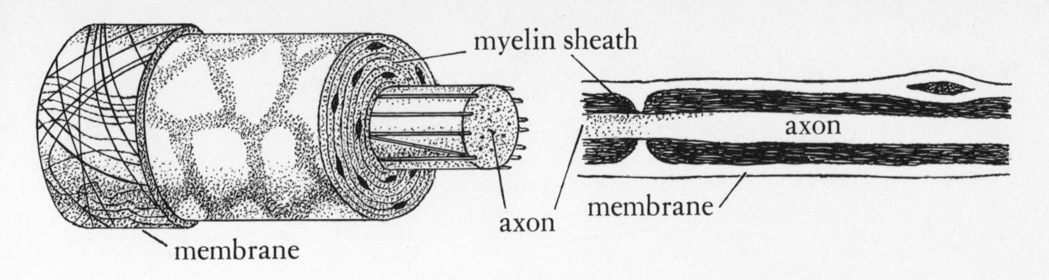

Most nerve fibers have a fatty, or myelin, sheath that aids in conducting nerve impulses. Some do not. The fatty covering is not complete at birth. It continues to develop all through childhood. The nerve fibers may not be completely sheathed in myelin until one is 16 or 17 years old.

The form and shape of nerve cells are varied. Some have few branches, but others, in the brain, have a maze of branches on the incoming side. Nerve endings sensitive to pain are relatively free and simple. Other endings that receive incoming sensations are specialized for their tasks. Those that are sensitive to taste, light, cold, or smell are very special indeed.

SOME SENSORY NERVE ENDINGS (very much enlarged)

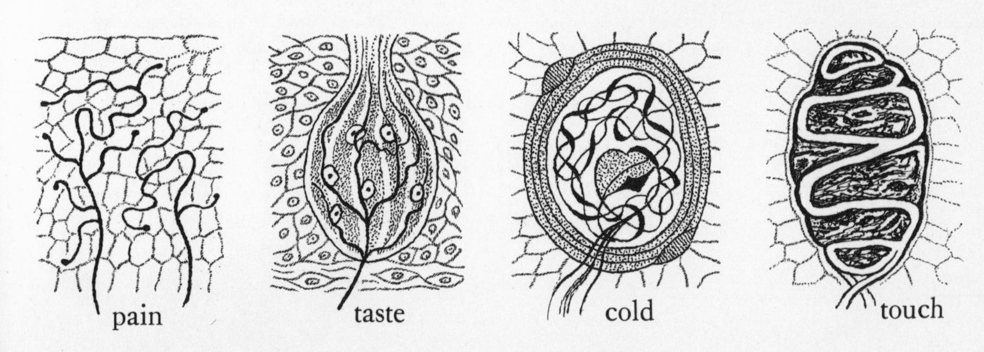

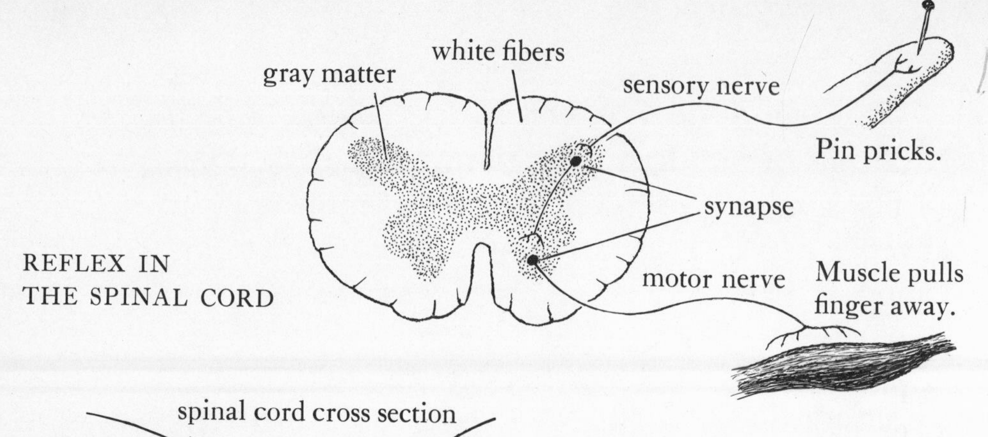

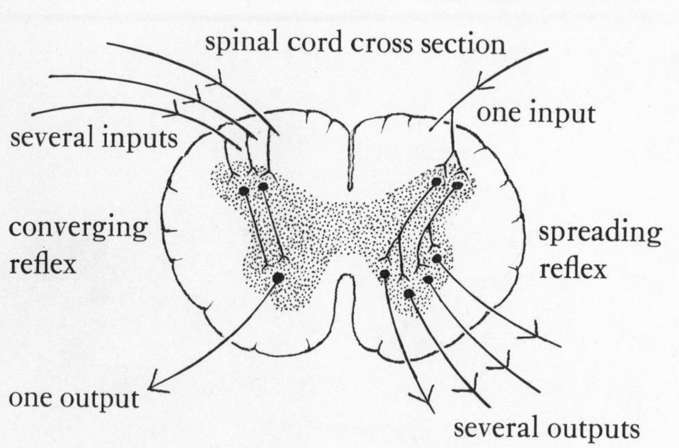

A reflex begins as something affecting the nerve fiber endings. Pain, heat, or pressure starts a chemical-electrical impulse in a nerve fiber. At the spinal cord, brain, or some other nerve center an output current starts action in muscles which withdraws the finger from possible danger.

Think of nerve cells as part of a battery circuit that makes electricity by chemical means, like that of a flashlight. The chemistry differs from a battery's, and, of course, the scale is much smaller. The amount of electricity in a nerve circuit is minute, but still sufficient to get messages rapidly around your body. If you touch a hot pan, your brain will know it in about 1/25 of a second, since most nerve impulses travel about 350 feet per second.

No single nerve cell works alone. Often dozens or hundreds take part in simple actions. The simplest of such actions is a reflex. The reflex may use as few as two nerve cells to get action. Usually a good many more are involved. All animals with nerves have reflexes—and people, too. Have you tried *not* to blink when someone waves a hand near your eye? When you touch something hot or sharp, you jerk your finger away. These are reflex actions.

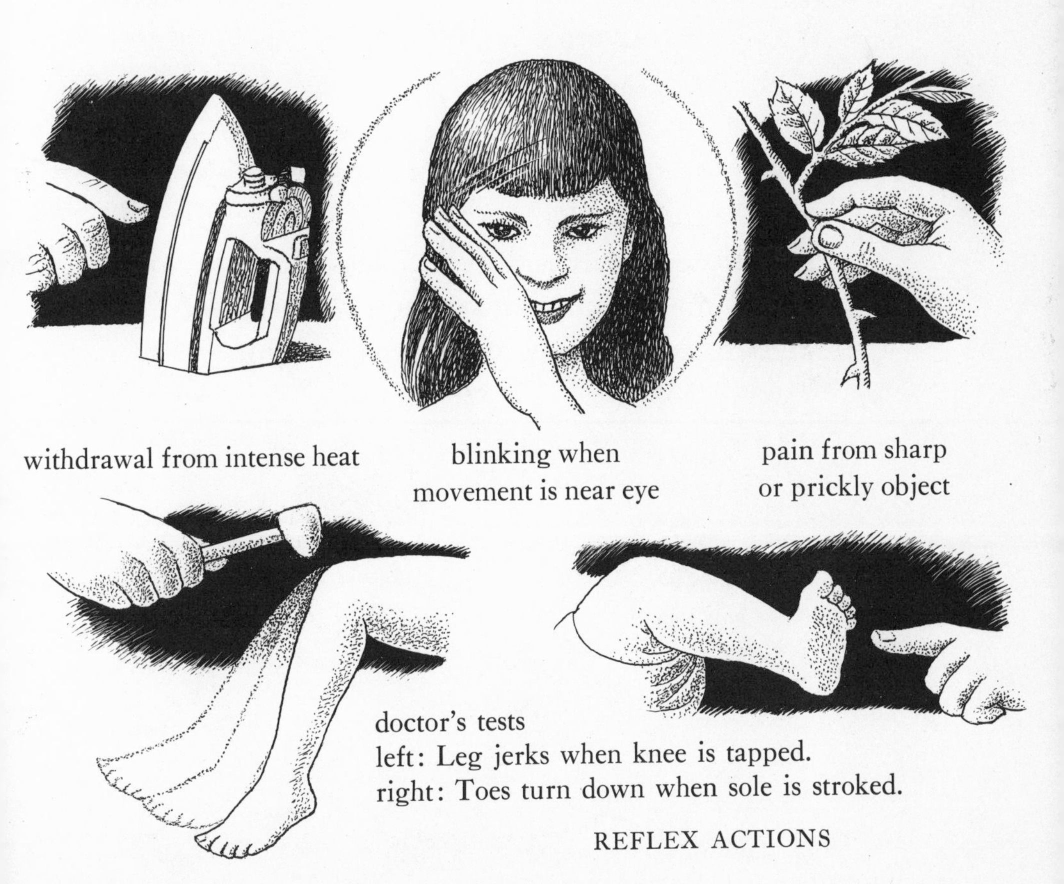

withdrawal from intense heat

blinking when movement is near eye

pain from sharp or prickly object

doctor's tests
left: Leg jerks when knee is tapped.
right: Toes turn down when sole is stroked.

REFLEX ACTIONS

But your brain may exercise control over some reflex actions if you want it to. When you go to the doctor to get a shot, you know he is going to stick a sharp needle in your arm. So you ask your brain to take control, and you don't jerk your arm away as you would if someone stuck you without warning. Many, but not all, reflexes are subject to such restraint through control exercised by your brain.

Actually, a reflex is not simple. You jerk away when something hurts you, but you also may jerk away in advance if you see what is coming. If you feel a sharp pain, you may do several things at the same time—jerk away your arm, turn your body to see what is happening, let out a cry. Tears may come to your eyes. Each of these actions involves different sets of nerves and muscles, but they all can happen within a second or so, before you know what went wrong.

Brain control can override a reflex as when a doctor gives an innoculation.

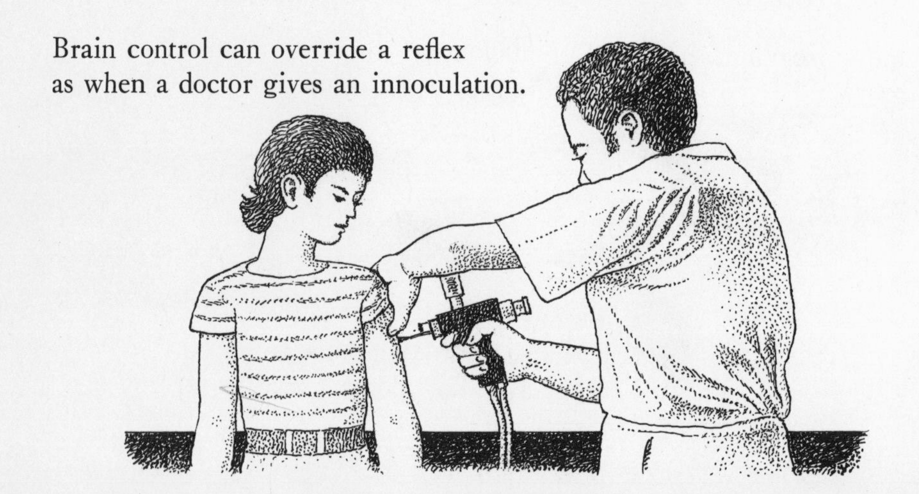

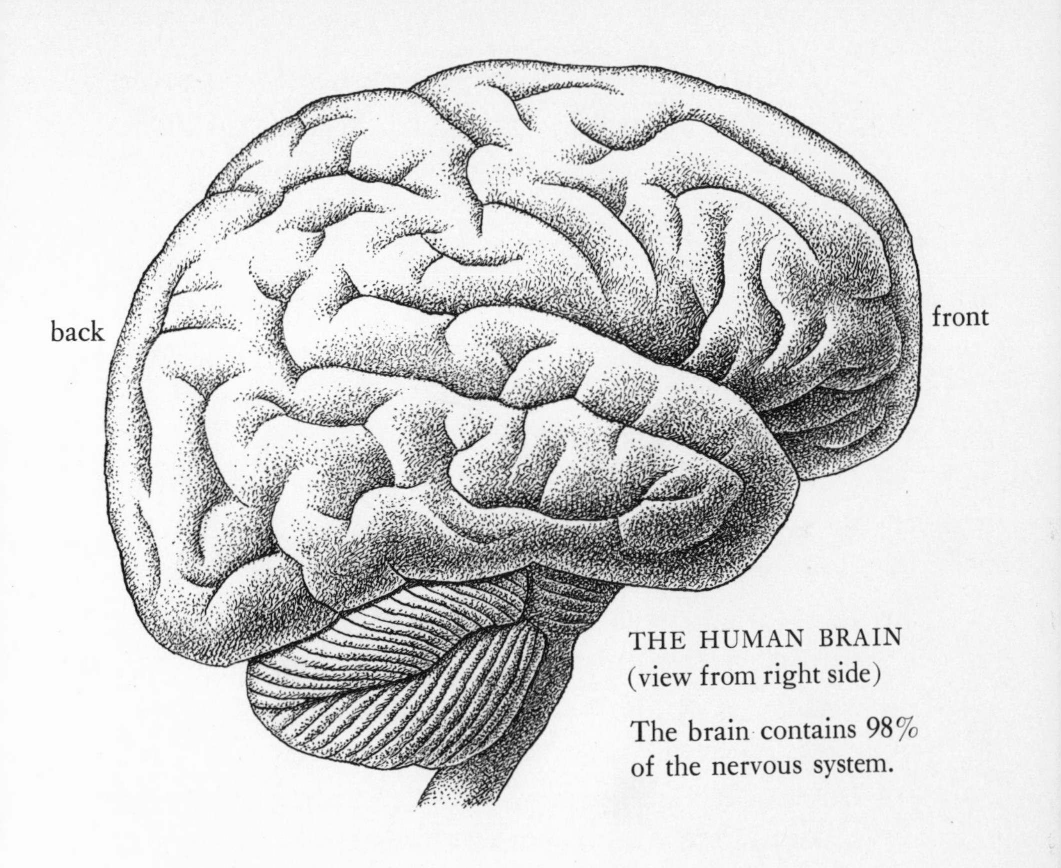

THE HUMAN BRAIN
(view from right side)

The brain contains 98% of the nervous system.

Billions of nerve cells make up the nervous system in which the brain is the most important organ. There is nothing quite like the human brain. It has made man the dominant living animal. Your brain controls, organizes, and protects your body. It keeps muscles ready for speedy action, maintains your posture and balance, and sets a pattern for movement. All these things are done without your awareness.

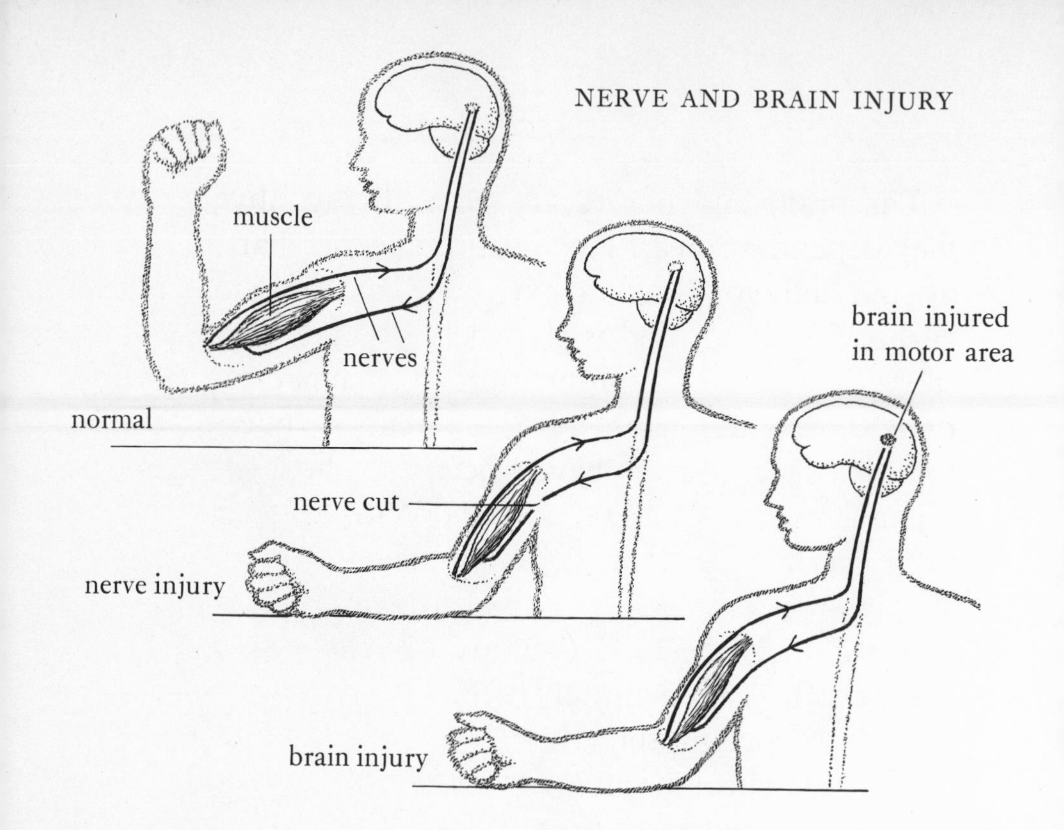

Your brain also works closely with the endocrine glands that produce action by means of chemical messages. Danger, fear, or anger, for example, alerts both the endocrine and the nervous system for your protection. Messages to and from the brain travel through the spinal cord and nerves that go to all parts of your body. If the nerves to an arm are cut, no action of the brain can make the arm move. The reverse is true also. A brain injury at the proper spot will paralyze an arm as completely as a cut nerve.

The brain and nerves are alive. Being alive they depend on nearby cells and on other parts of your body for food and oxygen. That the brain and nerves need food is shown by the fact that starvation or even malnutrition in young children affects their brain and intelligence. Undernourished children have been studied in Uganda, Mexico, and Guatemala. Within a year or so after birth they begin to develop more slowly than children who live nearby but are better fed. By the time they are of school age, these children are definitely behind the others.

Well-fed people sometimes think that certain foods have special value for the brain. Fish is often mentioned as an example of "brain food." The brain does need a good supply of food and oxygen, but it does not need any special food. A well-balanced diet, with variety, supplies the food chemicals, especially the proteins and sugars, that the brain needs.

Children who lack protein food may develop *kwashiorkor*, a disease that also may affect their brain.

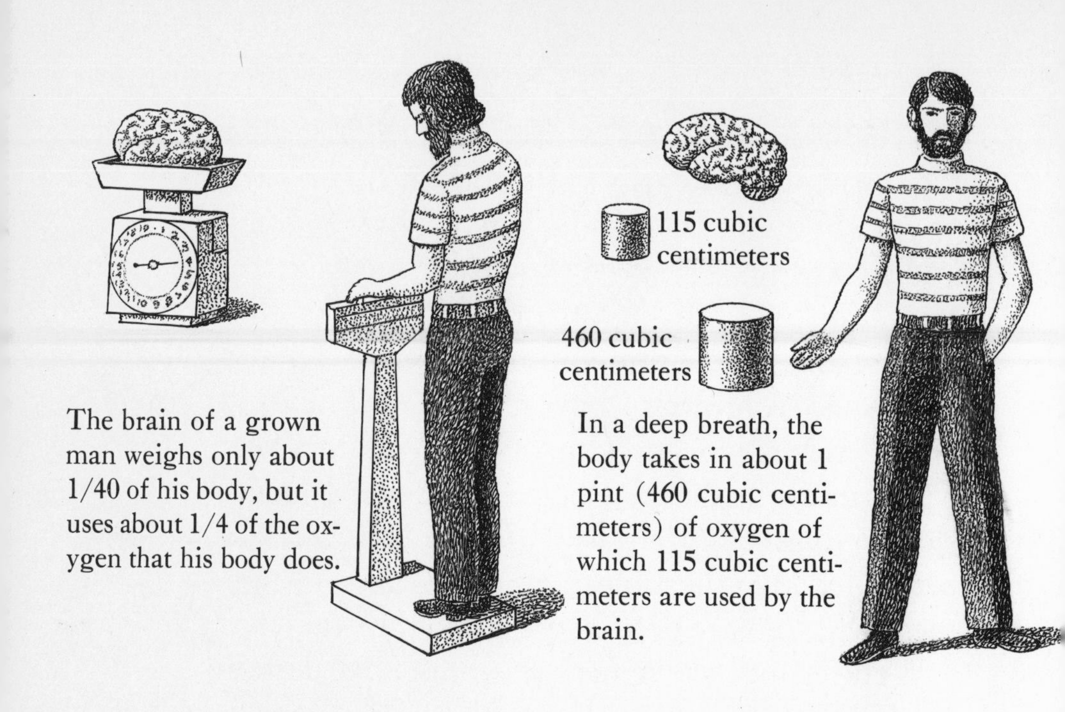

The brain of a grown man weighs only about 1/40 of his body, but it uses about 1/4 of the oxygen that his body does.

In a deep breath, the body takes in about 1 pint (460 cubic centimeters) of oxygen of which 115 cubic centimeters are used by the brain.

The effect of lack of oxygen on the brain is more drastic. While the brain and nerves of a grown man weigh only about one fortieth of his body weight, they use about one quarter of his oxygen intake. If the air supply is cut off for even three to five minutes, brain cells can be severely damaged. Even if breathing is restored, the brain may not recover from the injury. When breathing stops because of drowning, electric shock, or any other cause, try to start it again at once. Send for a doctor or police to provide emergency help.

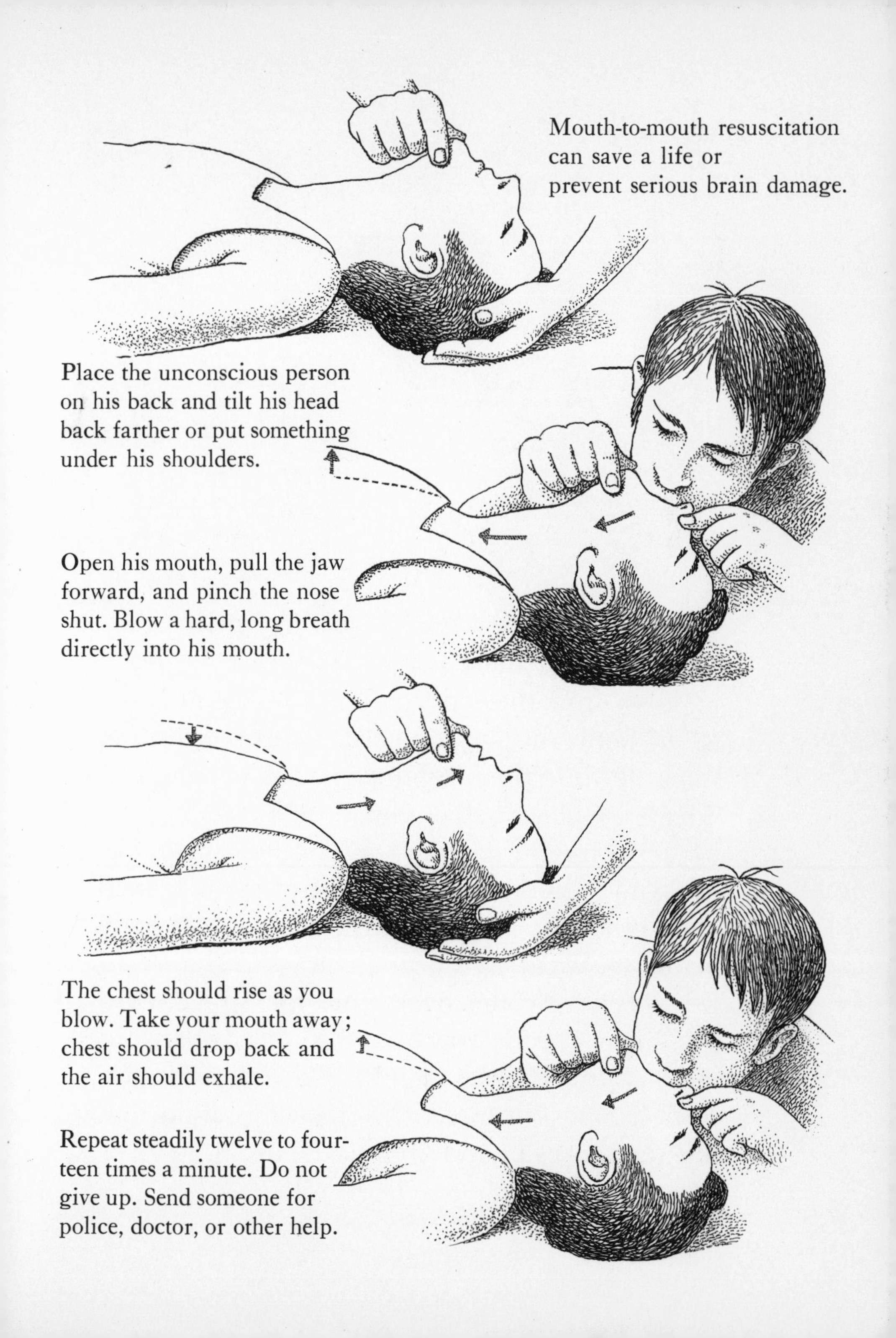

Mouth-to-mouth resuscitation can save a life or prevent serious brain damage.

Place the unconscious person on his back and tilt his head back farther or put something under his shoulders.

Open his mouth, pull the jaw forward, and pinch the nose shut. Blow a hard, long breath directly into his mouth.

The chest should rise as you blow. Take your mouth away; chest should drop back and the air should exhale.

Repeat steadily twelve to fourteen times a minute. Do not give up. Send someone for police, doctor, or other help.

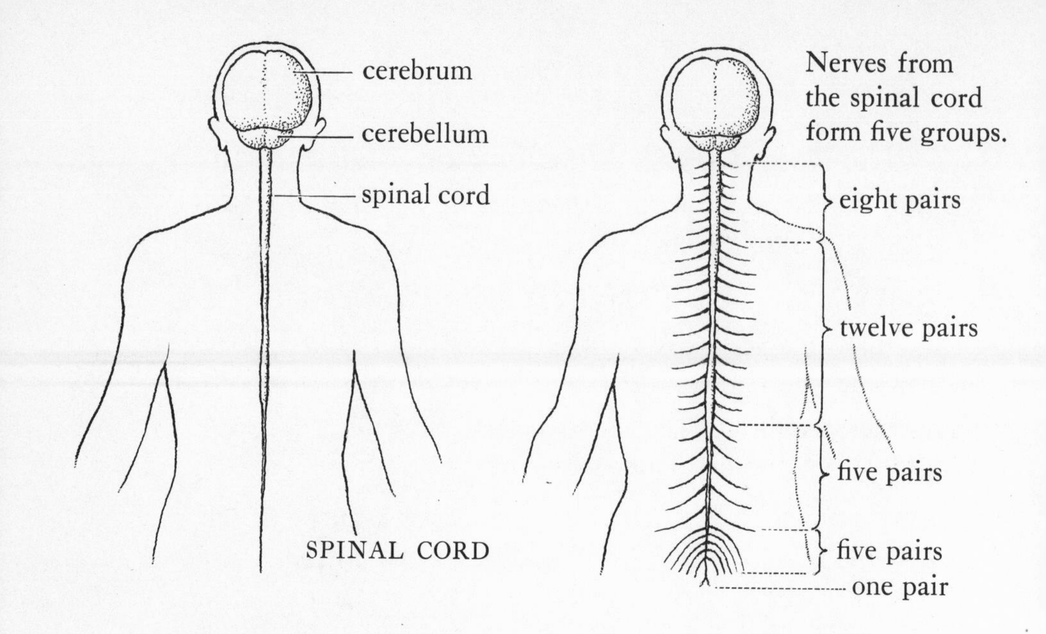

The spinal cord is the connecting link between the brain and most nerves. It forms the main pathway from the body to the brain and the brain to the body. The spinal cord leaves your brain, thick as your thumb, but tapers down rapidly. About 18 inches below the brain, it ends in your backbone as a fine thread. From the spinal cord 31 pairs of nerves extend. Most of them branch and branch again, going to all parts of the body below the head.

Protected by the backbone, the spinal cord gets further protection from membranes between the nerves and the bones. These membranes form a long sac filled with the same fluid that fills the spaces in and around the brain.

The spinal cord, an extension of the brain, has the same general appearance as that of brain tissue. Parts are gray; parts are white. The gray matter is in the interior. When cut across, it has a shape like the letter *H*. Surrounding this gray matter are the white nerve fibers, which branch within and from the spinal cord. These nerve fibers form a series of tracts. Those coming in and up to the brain are the sensory tracts. Those going down and out of the cord to muscles are the motor tracts.

The once-dread polio, or infantile paralysis, is a disease that attacks the spinal cord. The virus of this disease destroys the motor nerves. The brain may send a message to raise the left leg. But if the nerves carrying that message to the muscles of your thigh have been injured by polio, the message does not get through. The leg does not move. We say it is paralyzed.

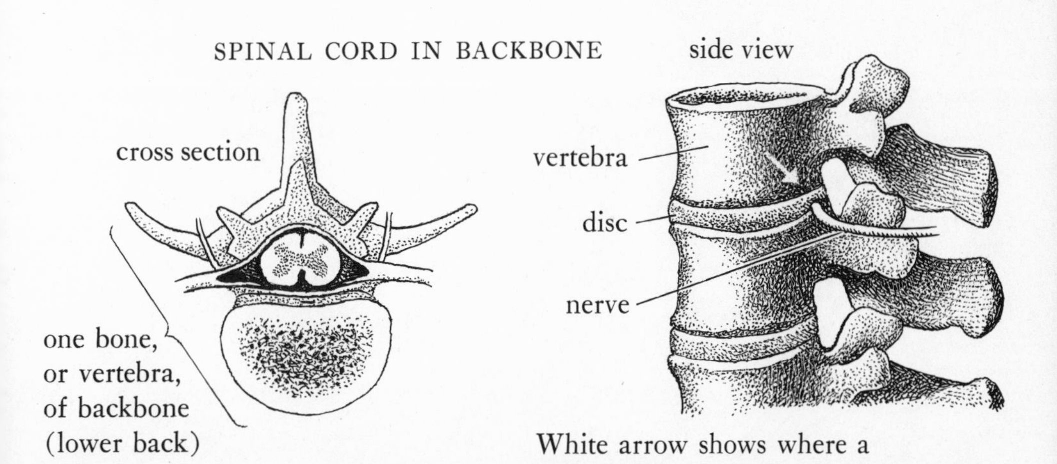

White arrow shows where a "slipped disc" can press upon a nerve.

In the small human embryo the neural plate and tube become both the brain and the spinal cord. Both form at about the same time, and one is not the outgrowth of the other. We speak of the spinal cord as the main connection to the brain. It is. But at the same time it is part of the brain.

Doctors often talk about the brainstem. This term usually means those old parts of the brain that still grow in segments—the hindbrain, the midbrain, the forebrain, and their parts. The stem is the core of the brain, and its parts are forward extensions of the spinal cord. The complete brain of fishes is no more than this simple brainstem.

Later came the development of the two larger and more important parts of the brain—the cerebellum and the cerebrum. The cerebellum

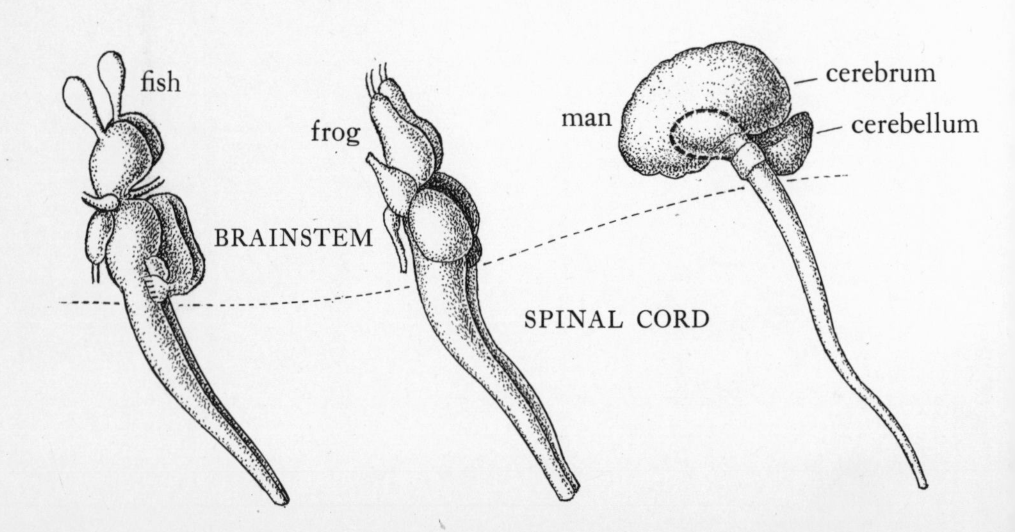

evolved from the front part of the old hindbrain. The cerebrum, the better-known thinking part of our brain, is an outgrowth of the old fore-brain. In the brains of frogs and reptiles these areas begin to be important. Mammals show a clear advance. The cerebrum of man over-whelms the rest of his brain.

The central nervous system includes the brain-stem, spinal cord, cerebellum, and cerebrum. Your body also has thousands of smaller nerves. Most of them are branches of the 31 pairs of spinal cord nerves. Other small nerves connect directly from the face and head to 12 pairs of cranial nerves that arise from the lower surface of the brain.

You also have another special and quite independent nervous system—the autonomic. It regulates important internal organs of your body.

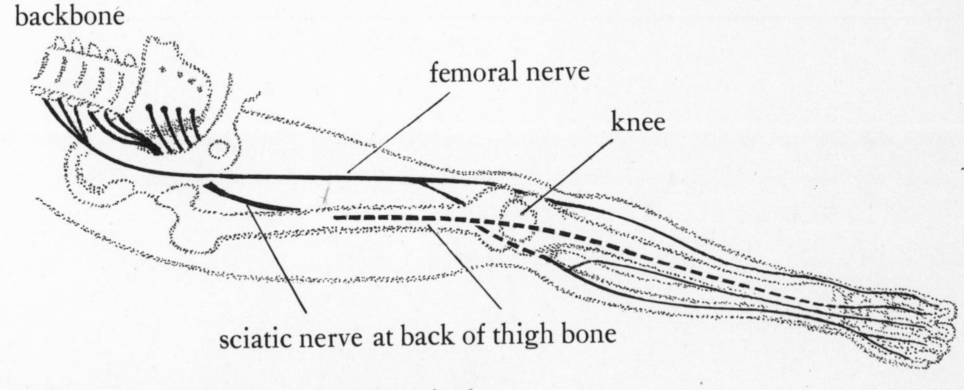

Nerves from the lower end of the spinal cord connect to the legs and feet. Hundreds of smaller nerves are not shown.

The upper end of the spinal cord passes through an opening into the skull and enters the brain. At once it thickens and spreads out. This wider, heavier part, known as the medulla, is part of the brain. It forms from the back of the old hindbrain and has nerves going directly to the mouth and face. As a part of the brain, the medulla does important things.

Many common reflexes make their connections through this part of the brain. When you cough or sneeze or swallow, the medulla is involved. It is also the area that makes you vomit when you are sick and thus protects your body by removing something that might be dangerous.

Other reflexes, which you do not feel or notice, act through the medulla also. They include reflexes that take part in the digestion of food. For example, the churning movements of your stomach and intestines mix food and move it through the 28 feet of your digestive tube.

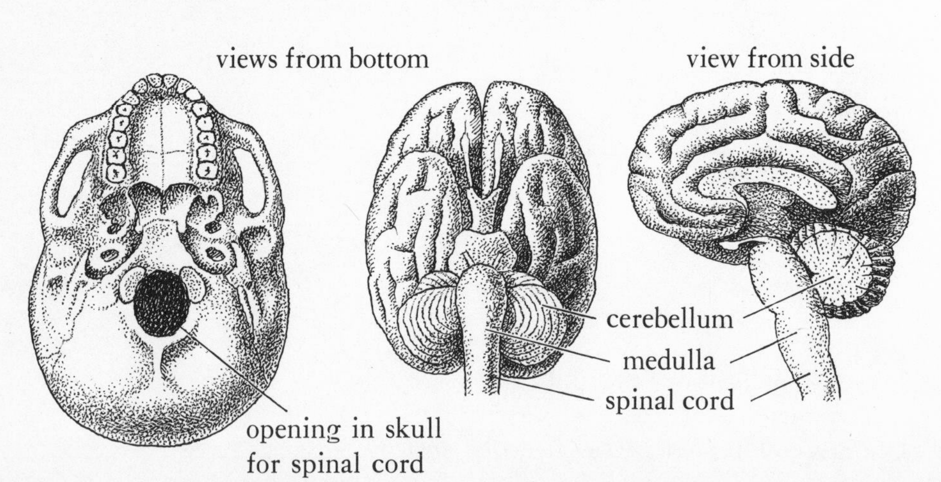

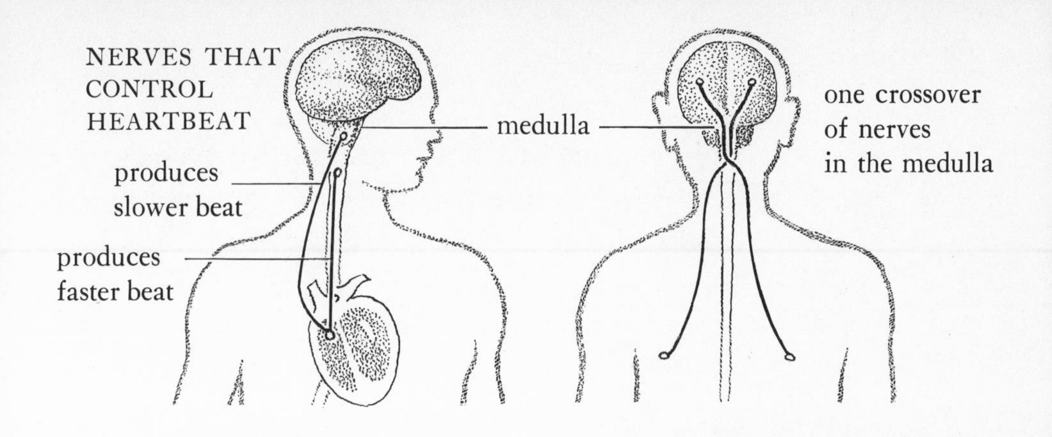

In addition, the medulla controls what doctors call the vital centers. One regulates the beating of your heart and keeps it from going too slow or too fast. A breathing center controls the rhythm of your lungs. You plunge into a cold lake and catch your breath as a response to signals from cold receptors. The carbon dioxide in your blood triggers the breathing center too. Thus, you breathe faster and deeper when the amount of carbon dioxide is high, as during strenuous play or very hard work.

The medulla is also the place where major motor nerve tracts cross. Those from the left side of the body go to the right side of the brain and vice versa. Lastly the medulla is a relay station, with many synapses, monitoring messages to and from your cerebrum and muscles. All these activities of your medulla go unnoticed, except when you cough or sneeze.

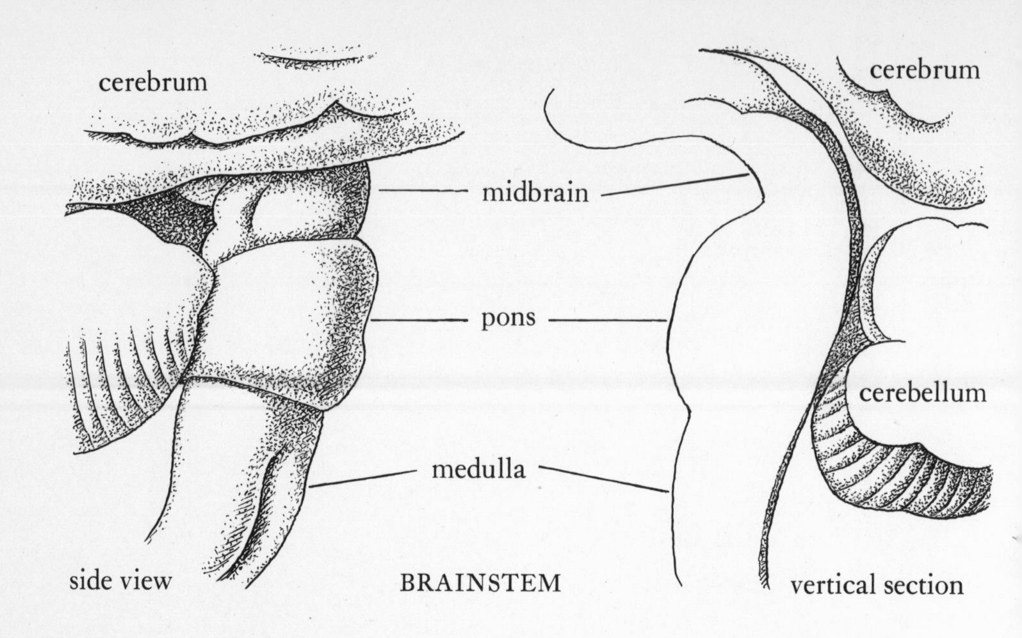

Above the medulla in the brainstem, and connecting it with the newer and larger parts of the brain is the area known as the pons. This small section ties together three major parts of the brain. It is also a place where nerves connect to your face and ears. One role of the pons is the control of breathing—something it shares with the medulla.

Near the pons is the small midbrain section, once larger and more important. It still acts in reflexes that begin with light and sound. In addition, it helps with muscle control and posture and has other functions, some of which are not very clear to us, in relaying messages.

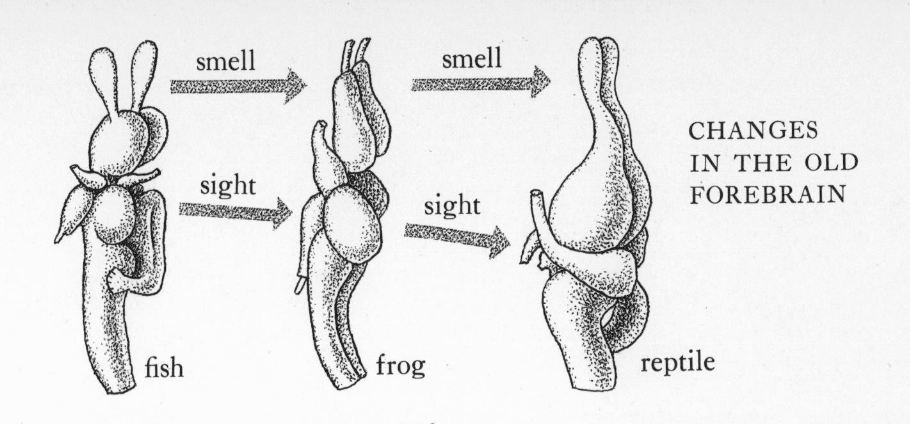

The front end of the brainstem is the forebrain. It seems almost lost, because our cerebrum has grown so large that the old forebrain is hidden within it. Long ago the forebrain was mainly concerned with smell—a basic sense for water animals. Other parts of the old forebrain also have lost some of their importance. Among some reptiles one part (the pineal body) once functioned as a third eye.

Now the thalamus of the forebrain serves as a relay center for many incoming messages, especially those about heat and cold, pain and touch. It supports the cerebrum in making you conscious and aware.

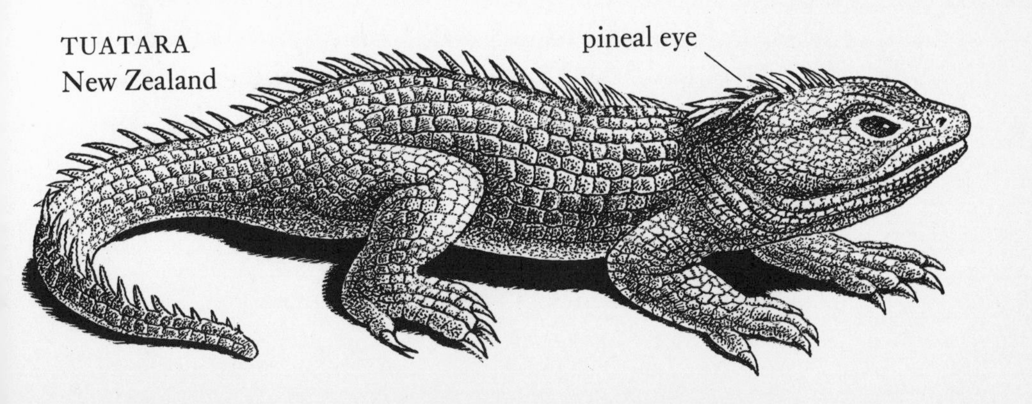

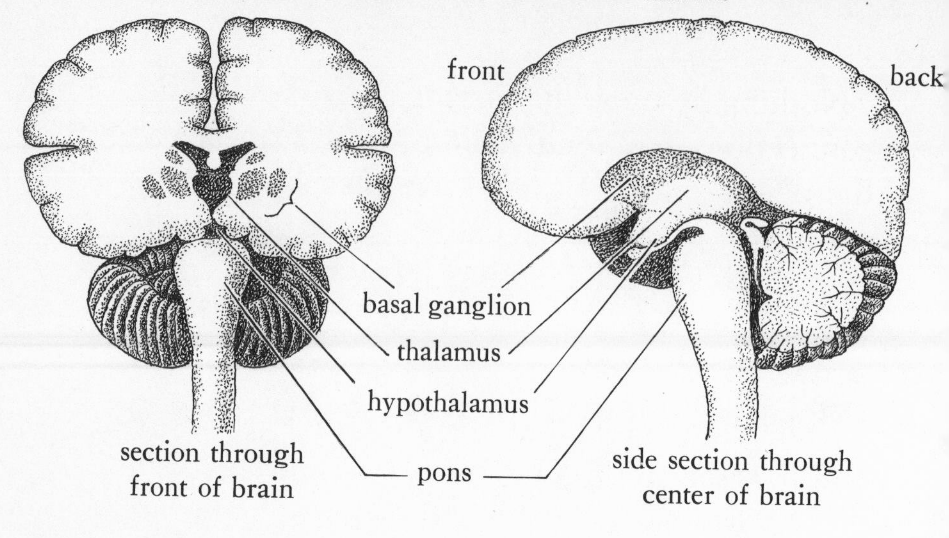

Below is the small hypothalamus concerned with temperature control and the regulation of internal affairs like water balance. Much of this work is done by means of your autonomic nervous system. Experiments show the hypothalamus is tied in with emotions like fear, anger, and rage. It regulates appetite and hunger and also may influence sleeping and waking.

All through the upper brainstem nerve fibers run in every direction, making connections that are hard to follow. One area, the basal ganglion, aids in supporting muscle tone and patterns of movement. It has connections with the cerebrum and the cerebellum—the newer parts of the brain.

Nothing is more important than these many connections between the old primitive brain and the new thinking brain. They may also be the cause, or part of the cause, of some serious mental diseases. Recently a new kind of brain surgery uses radioactive or heat needles to destroy some connecting areas in the brains of very sick people. This may prevent messages of fear, rage, or anger from taking control of their brain and producing violent behavior.

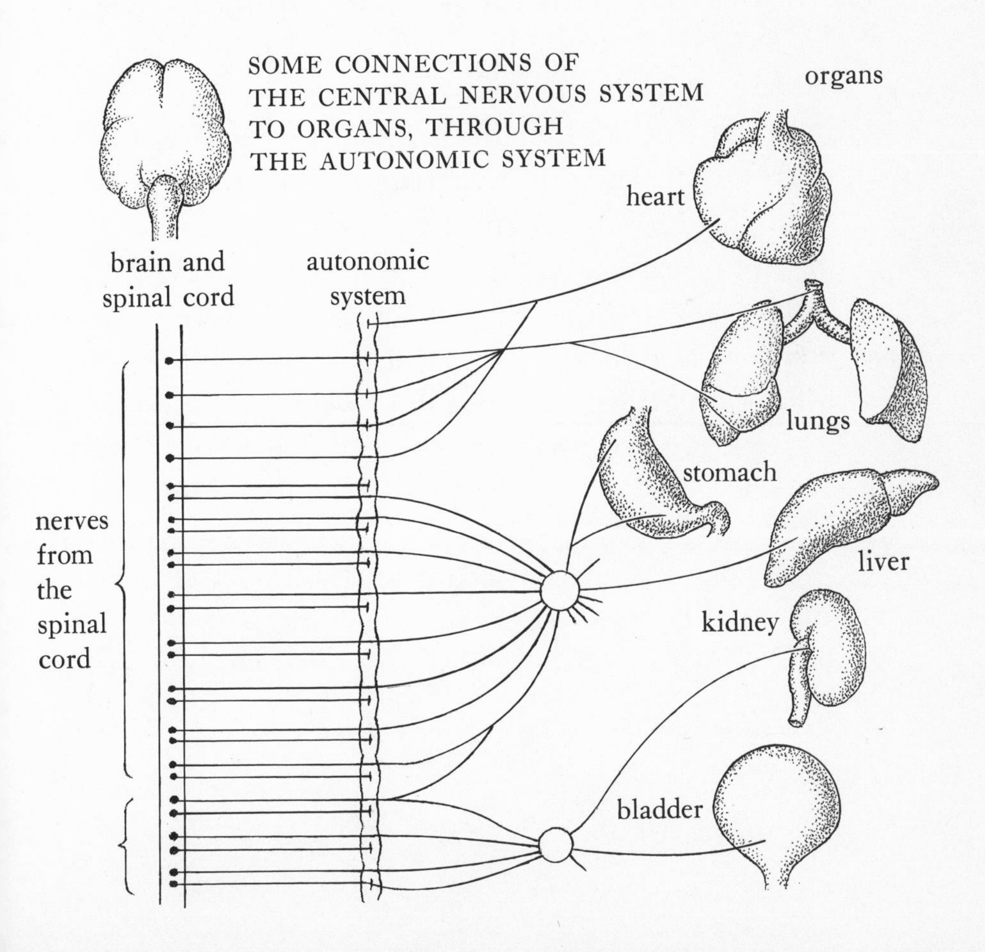

For nearly 500 million years the old brainstem has shown its worth in backboned animals. It controls many actions essential to life itself. Yet we often do not think of these tasks as brain work. Because the older brainstem does its work so well, newer brain parts have been able to develop and take on additional tasks. A new part of the brain does not perform the same work as an old part. It often refines and modifies the action and provides much better control.

Two newer parts of the brain have developed in backboned animals. They are such important areas that they are called the brain proper, in contrast to the older brainstem. The first is the cerebellum, an oval, constricted, furrowed area at the back of the brain. In it, the gray matter is on the outside and the white nerve fibers are a tight mass within. This structure is just the opposite of that of the spinal cord. The cerebellum, folded very tightly, contains a great deal of nerve tissue in a very small space.

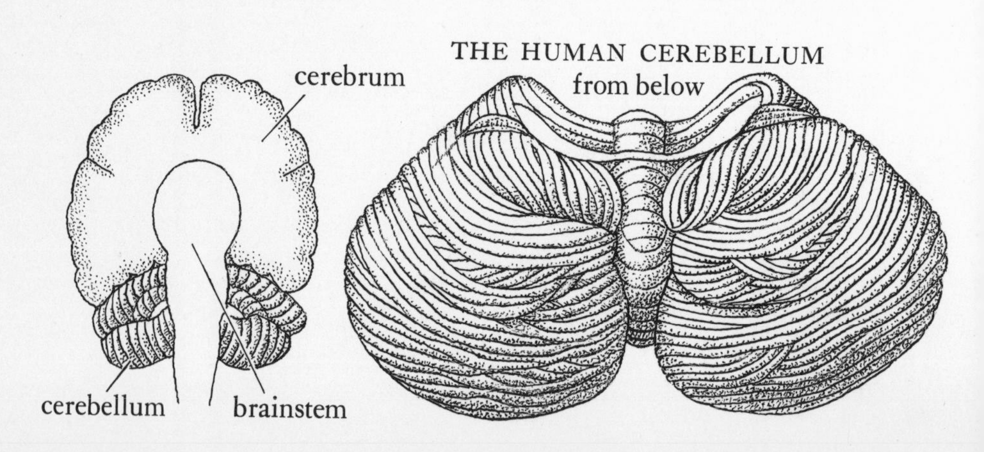

THE HUMAN CEREBELLUM
from below

The cerebellum has been compared to the digital computer, the kind used widely today. This type operates via an on-off signal, which pulses like a nerve current. Digital computers are high speed, accurate, compact, and suited to problems of logic and control.

When a new high-speed digital model was announced recently, its makers were reminded of a common model, already available, that could handle more complex problems and store more information—the human brain.

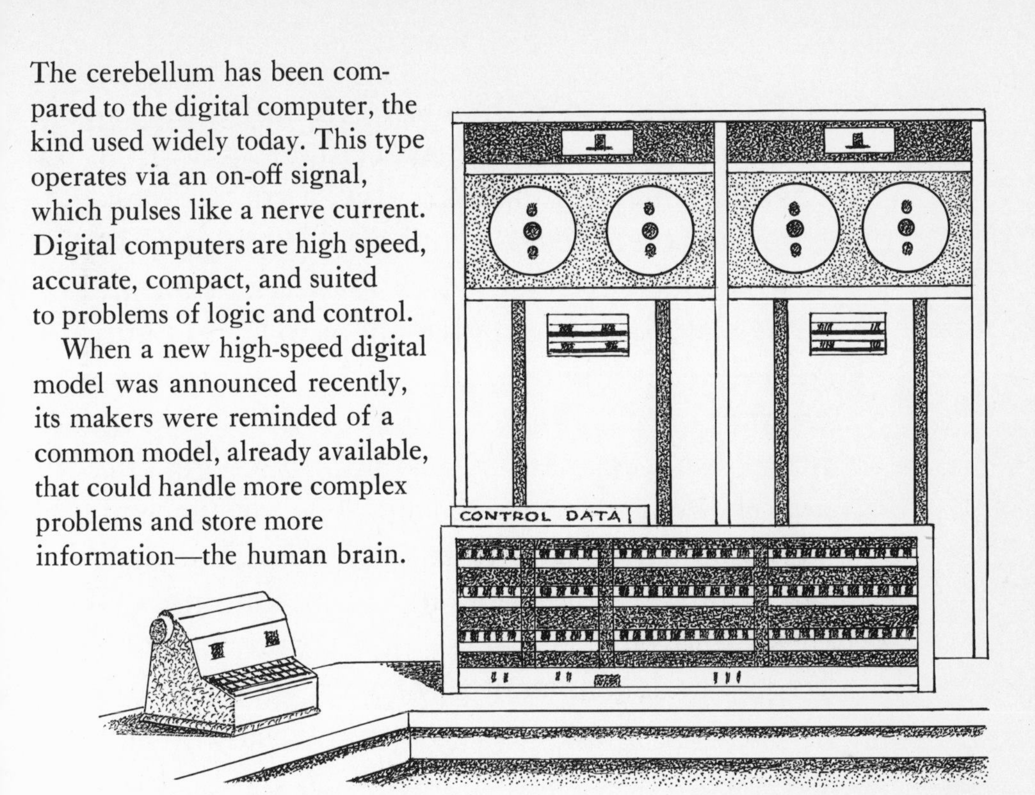

Although the brain is far more complex than the best computer, the cerebellum does have a computer pattern of action. Computers do not think or make decisions. Neither does the cerebellum. Computers store a tremendous amount of information. This information can be pulled together in many ways, for many different purposes. The cerebellum can do the same thing when you use any of your 639 muscles in any combination.

An example: you are playing tag. Someone is chasing you. As you run on the lawn you see in front of you a hedge about two feet high. You must decide quickly whether to turn and run the other way, to stop and give up, or to try to jump. You decide to jump and speed up to make the effort. You change your body position, eye the hedge, and estimate your jump. You get into action for just the right leap. You stretch your legs, your arms, and turn your body. You land safely on the other side and keep running. All these movements were done automatically, largely under the control of your cerebellum.

In all such activities, you do not have to stop and figure out step by step what to do. Each necessary movement falls into place. Actions are blended together, and quickly too. This remarkable ability began when you learned to crawl, to walk, to run, to jump.

The cerebellum helps muscles to work together.

BALLET PRACTICE BAR (an example of muscle control and learning)

At first you did these important things slowly and clumsily. You fell down, missed the mark, and sometimes you got hurt. But after a while, as the muscle patterns became fixed in your brain, things went much better. As soon as you started to run, the movements came in the right order, at the right time, without your thinking about them.

Muscle learning is controlled largely by the cerebellum. When you try a new exercise, game, or activity, your first movements will be awkward. After a while you "get the feel." You stop thinking because your cerebellum has taken over the coordination of dozens of muscles. Your mind is no longer muscle-bound.

These kinds of things, once learned, are done almost automatically. You improve with training or practice, since muscle activity does not require much thinking. This improvement depends on several levels in your brain. The thinking part provides the final monitoring and the delicate balance that makes control precise.

A top athlete has well-developed muscles and fine muscle control. But his thinking brain is also alert for every opportunity in the sport. He makes good decisions quickly and carries them through. That ability is what puts him at the top and makes him a star.

The cerebellum and cerebrum give the control needed in sports.

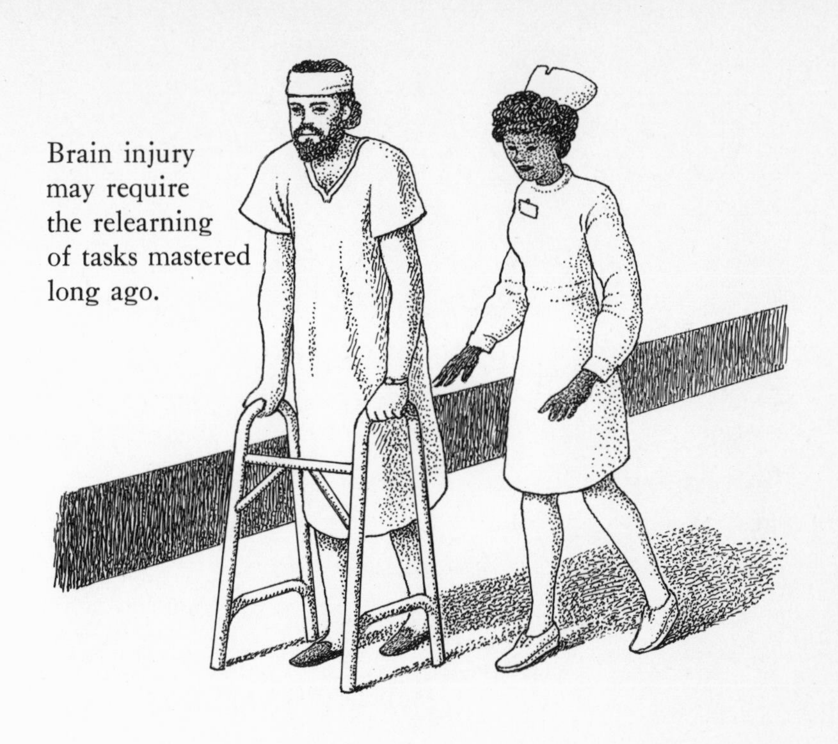

Brain injury may require the relearning of tasks mastered long ago.

Very rarely a person has an injury or disease that affects his cerebellum. Such a person is able to think about what he wants to do. He can decide on some action, such as walking across the room or lacing his shoes, but his muscles do not follow through automatically. The movements he makes are jerky. Sometimes an arm will go out too far, or a leg will stop short. The simplest task becomes one that can be performed only slowly and with difficulty. Repeated decisions are needed to make correction after correction of errors, due to lack of control and coordination.

Many activities are automatic or nearly so.

Since much of your life is spent doing things automatically (eating, walking, reading), the cerebellum is extremely important. The work that you finish quickly and easily, the games you enjoy, the skills you develop through interest and practice, all come from the action of your cerebellum. Doing these things is certainly part of living happily. Every healthy person should be able to take them for granted, no matter what his schooling.

Without the cerebellum and the brain stem largely controlling the vital processes, routine tasks, and muscle coordination, your thinking brain would be busy with unimportant but essential details of living. It never could do all the other things that make the total brain so effective. Perhaps the most exciting thing about the brain is that all the parts, old and new, large and small, work so well together.

The thinking part of the brain—the cerebrum—has become so large we mistake it for the entire brain. Growing from the old forebrain, the cerebrum has become much more important to man than to all other animals. It is the pineapple-shaped part of the brain that takes up most of the space inside your skull. It makes up seven eighths of the brain's weight.

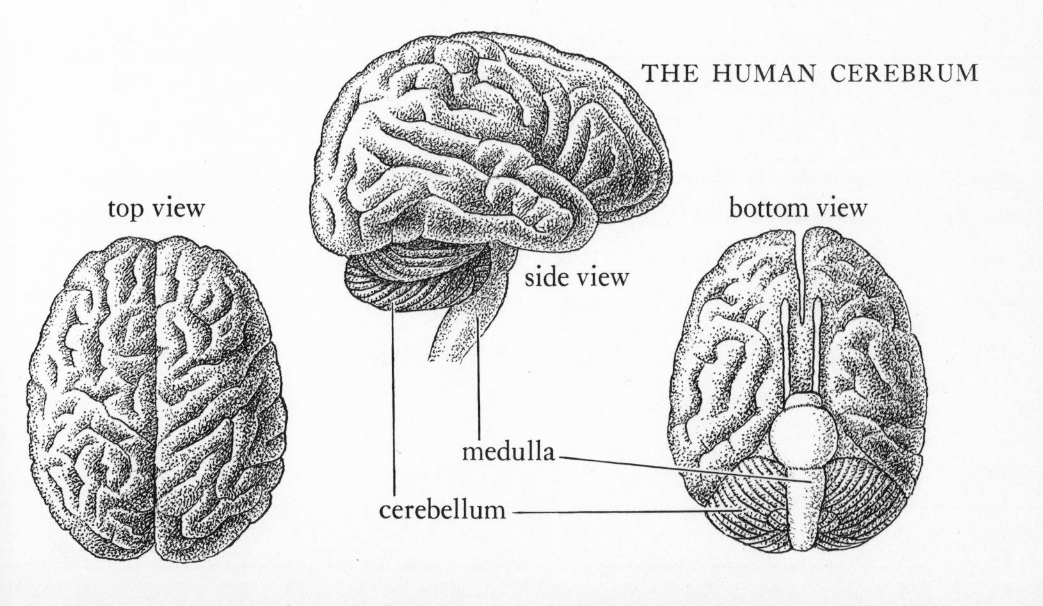

THE HUMAN CEREBRUM

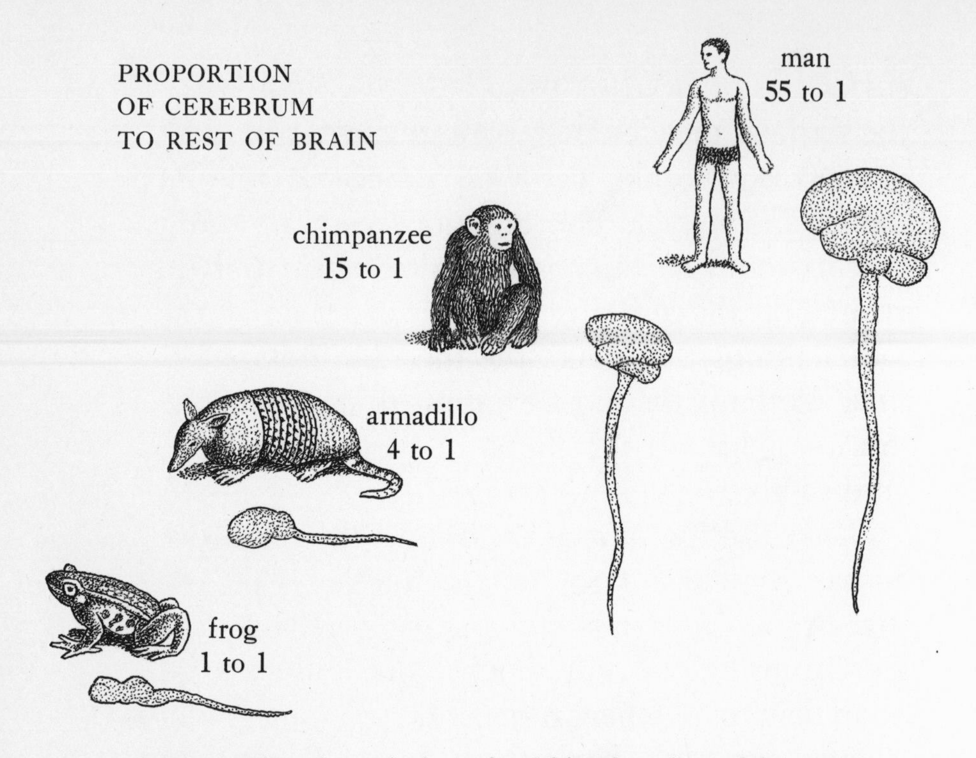

Progressing through the animal kingdom from fish to man, the cerebrum becomes more and more important.

Important as it is, the cerebrum works closely with the rest of the brain, through the cerebellum, stem, medulla, spinal cord, and all of the nervous system. It has many connections with other parts of the brain. Several parts of the old brain stem connect to and interconnect with the cerebrum and the cerebellum.

Although large, the cerebrum is still relatively unknown. When a surgeon looks at it, he sees a surface of ridges, furrows, clefts, and fissures. If the surface area were spread out smoothly, the cerebrum would be at least twice as big. Hence the wrinkles and furrows do an ideal job of getting a great deal of surface material into a small space.

The surface, or cortex, of the cerebrum is the gray matter, made up of about 10 billion nerve cells, or neurons, that do not have a fatty sheath. After middle age these die off at a rate of about 100,000 cells a day. By the time one is old, the brain may have lost a tenth of its cells. This may account for loss of memory and other signs of mental aging.

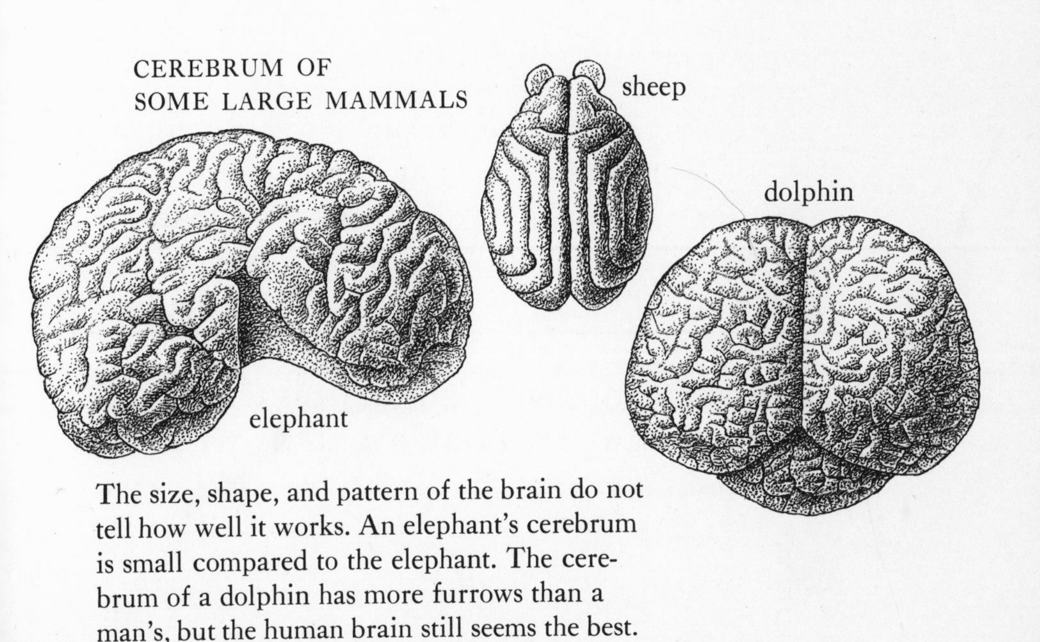

The size, shape, and pattern of the brain do not tell how well it works. An elephant's cerebrum is small compared to the elephant. The cerebrum of a dolphin has more furrows than a man's, but the human brain still seems the best.

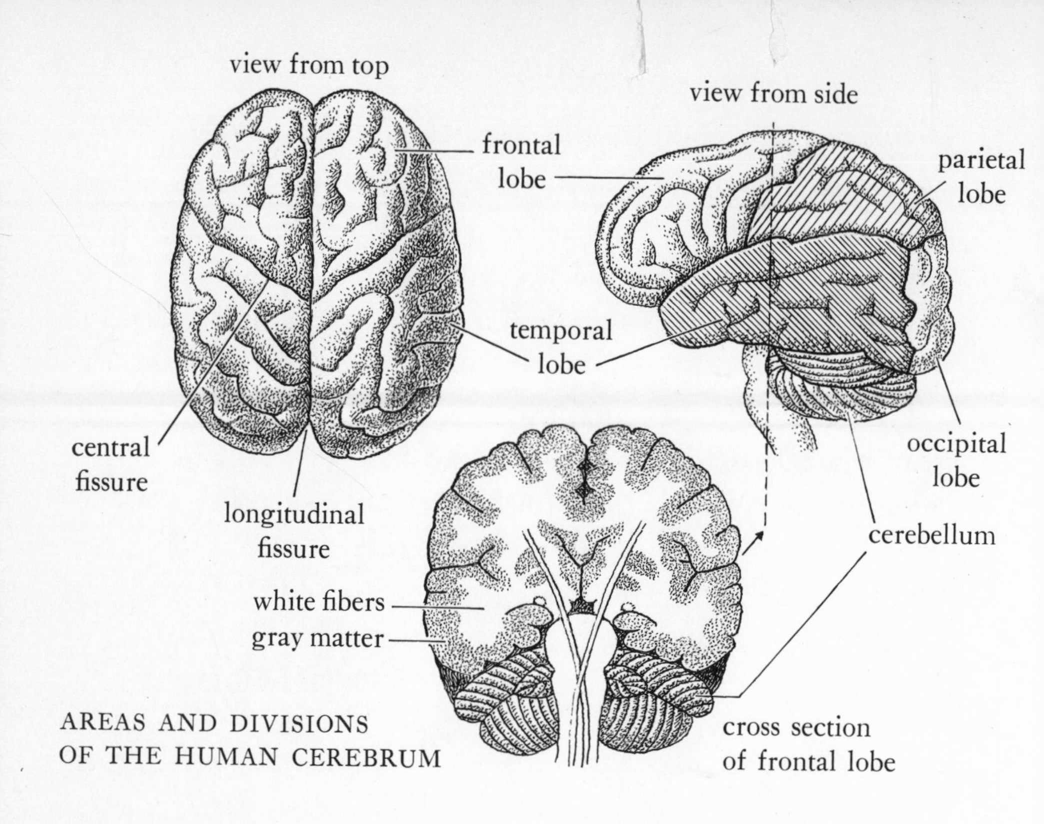

AREAS AND DIVISIONS OF THE HUMAN CEREBRUM

Inside the mass of gray matter is a central core of white fibers. One major fissure nearly divides the cerebrum into halves; another separates it from the cerebellum. From the top the cerebrum seems divided into quarters. From the side it is divided into four lobes. These divisions are not separate or distinct. The same is true of the cerebrum as a whole. While some parts do special jobs, much of the cerebrum works as an interconnected unit.

People once thought the cerebrum was divided into many small areas, each responsible for some activity or character trait. If a certain part of the brain were well developed, the corresponding ability or traits would be developed in that person also. The developed part of the cerebrum was expected to be larger, forming a bump, which, in turn, would produce a bump on the skull. A century or more ago people studied bumps on the skull to understand character and personality. Charts showed bumps for honesty, compassion, self-esteem, and other traits.

All this theory turned out to be fable, but it did have the good effect of promoting further study of the brain. Now scientists know there is no easy physical way to judge the brain. Neither bumps nor shape nor size indicates a person's intelligence or personality. A large brain is not better than a small one. Records show great men have had either.

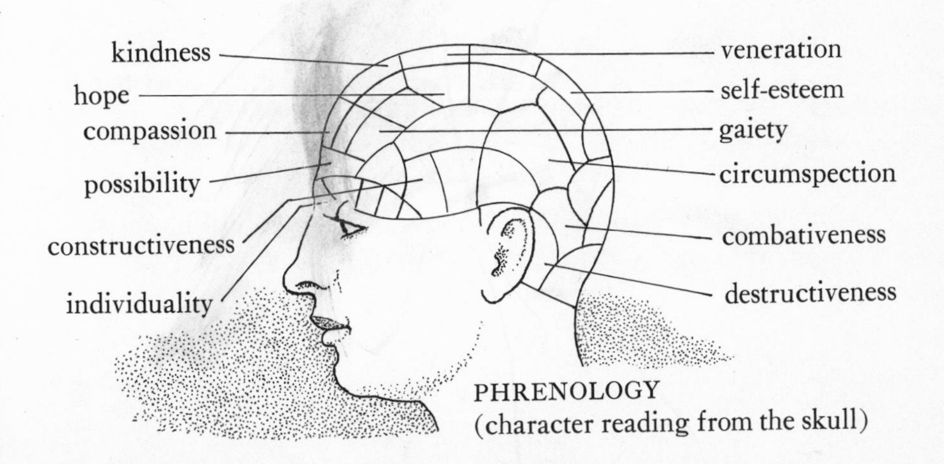

PHRENOLOGY
(character reading from the skull)

TWO GREAT AUTHORS WITH
BRAINS OF DIFFERENT SIZES

Anatole France: 1020 cubic centimeters   Ivan Turgenev: 2010 cubic centimeters

The average brain of an average man weighs about three pounds. Race or skin color makes no difference, but smaller people have relatively smaller brains. Women, generally smaller and lighter than men, have smaller brains also. On an average a woman's brain is about 10 percent, or one quarter pound, lighter than a man's, but it is just as good for thinking.

The shape of the head fixes the shape of the brain. Some heads are nearly round, some long and narrow. This difference has no effect on the brain either. Mothers in some primitive groups used to flatten a baby's skull to make it more attractive. This treatment affected the shape, but not the function of the brain.

While much of the cerebrum works as a whole, just how it works is not too clear. It is the part of the brain that does the work of association—of bringing all kinds of thoughts and ideas together. It makes use of intelligence, of reason, of memory, of conscience. Messages from the senses like those of hearing, smell, and taste are passed up to the cerebrum, which tells you what they mean. The cerebrum is the part of the brain that interprets the world around you.

The cerebrum orders and organizes all the things you do because you want to do them. Even such a simple task as reading and understanding these lines is controlled by your cerebrum. However, the mechanics of reading, such as the movements of your eyes, the flipping of the pages, are aided and controlled by the cerebellum and the brainstem.

Flathead Indians deformed the skull, but this practice had no effect on the working of the brain.

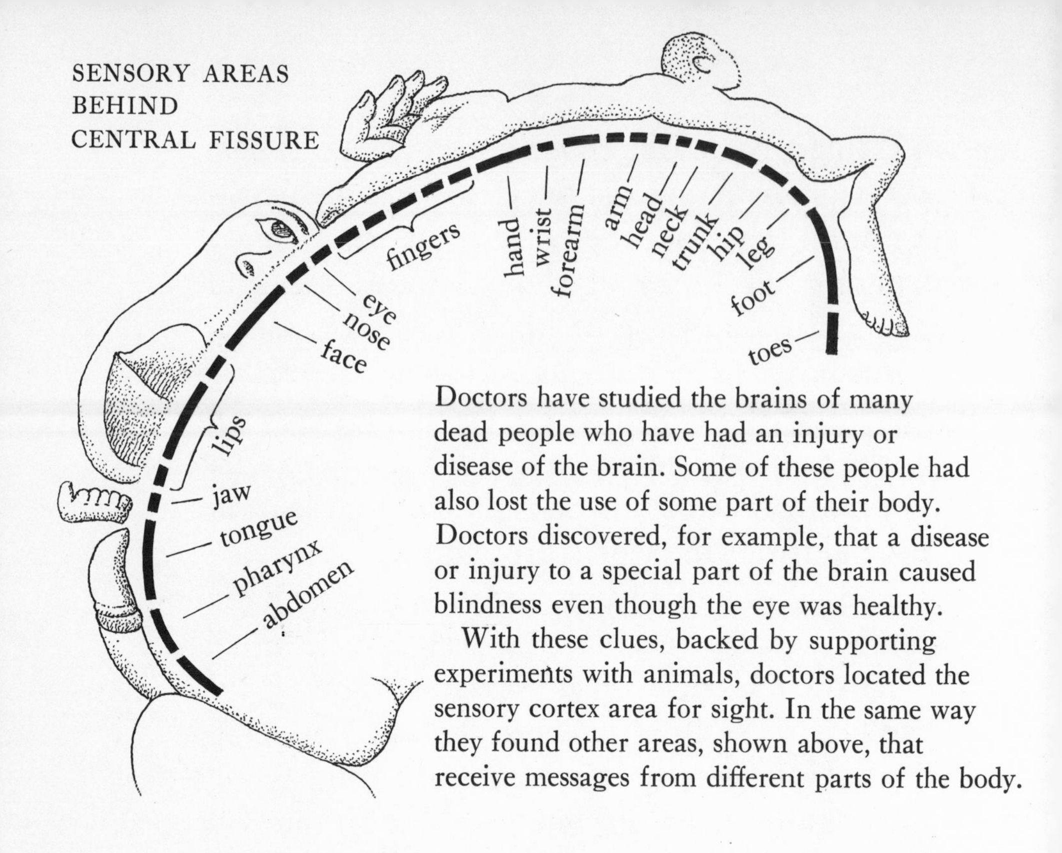

Doctors have studied the brains of many dead people who have had an injury or disease of the brain. Some of these people had also lost the use of some part of their body. Doctors discovered, for example, that a disease or injury to a special part of the brain caused blindness even though the eye was healthy.

With these clues, backed by supporting experiments with animals, doctors located the sensory cortex area for sight. In the same way they found other areas, shown above, that receive messages from different parts of the body.

The cortex, or outer gray matter, of the cerebrum does have some important local areas. Outstanding are those on either side of the central fissure. Behind and along one side of this fissure are a series of localized sensory spots that receive incoming impulses. These impulses are received in the areas shown below. Each is a center for messages from body parts that are illustrated. Some parts of the body need and have connections to larger sensory areas than others.

Opposite these sensory areas, on the front side of the central fissure, are a series of motor areas. They are similar but not exactly the same as the sensory areas. These paired sensory and motor areas are found on both sides, or hemispheres, of the brain. This arrangement raises the interesting but difficult question of duplication of work in the brain. In some cases one area backs up another. In the cerebral motor areas nerves of one side control muscles on the opposite side of the body. An injury to the right side of the head may paralyze a left arm or leg.

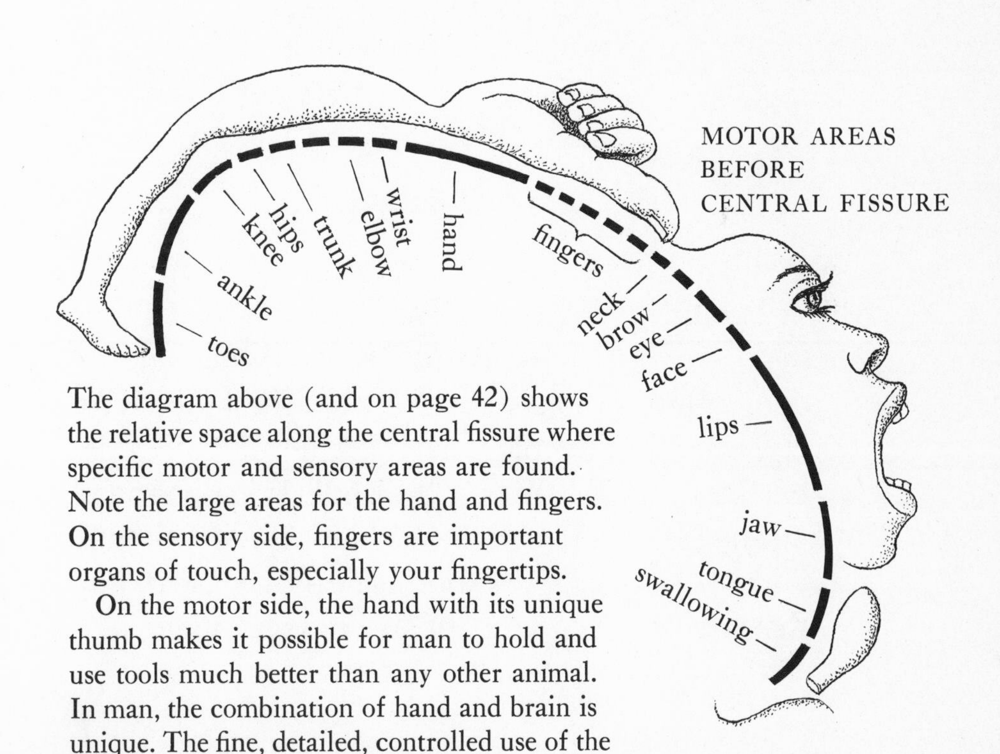

The diagram above (and on page 42) shows the relative space along the central fissure where specific motor and sensory areas are found. Note the large areas for the hand and fingers. On the sensory side, fingers are important organs of touch, especially your fingertips.

On the motor side, the hand with its unique thumb makes it possible for man to hold and use tools much better than any other animal. In man, the combination of hand and brain is unique. The fine, detailed, controlled use of the fingers comes from the cerebrum.

Your brain determines if you
are right- or left-handed.
If the left cerebrum is dominant,
your right hand is likely to be so.

Though both sides of the cerebrum look alike, they are not actually the same. One side is dominant and takes control over the other. For right-handed people, the left side of the brain takes control. Experts still wonder what happens on the side of the cerebrum that is not dominant. They believe that it is not useless or wasted, but that it helps the dominant side to coordinate.

The speech area seems to be found only in the dominant half of the cerebrum. But if that area is destroyed by accident or disease, the same area on the other side of the brain may take over in a young person. Thus speech may be relearned slowly. But this process does not happen all of the time or to the same degree.

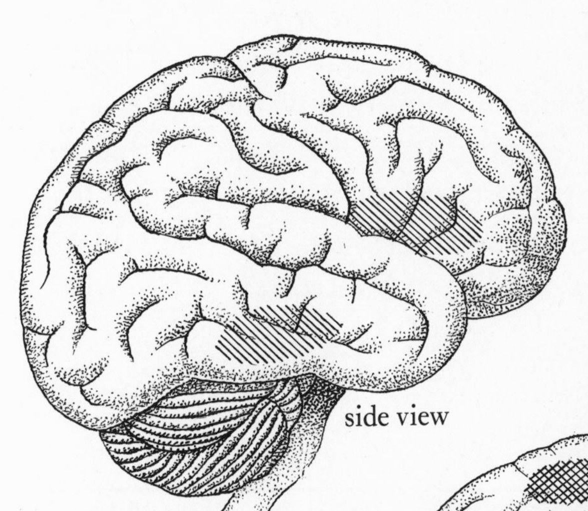

side view

SPEECH AREAS

possible or dormant speech areas shown with slanting lines

active speech areas shown with crossed lines

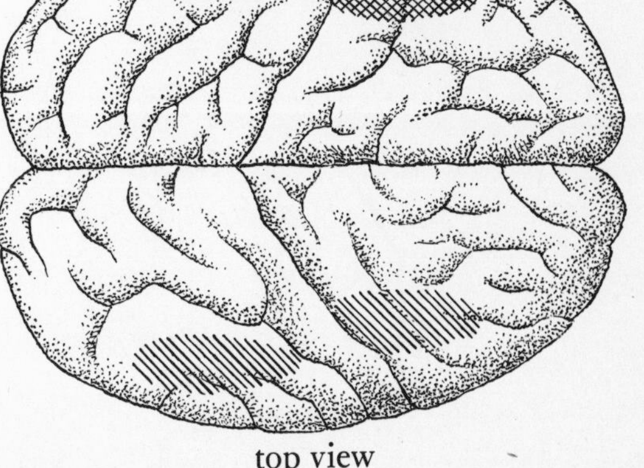

top view

The areas shown here are only part of the mechanism for speech. Sounds have to be made and then transformed into words. The meaning of words is learned and remembered. Speech requires nerve connections of brain, lips, tongue, throat, and face. Now add the knowledge and experience of the mind (pages 55-63) to set up patterns of written and spoken communication.

Injury to a part of the motor cortex at birth may produce the uncontrolled spastic movements of cerebral palsy. This term also is applied to other motor diseases. All are being studied in the hope of finding prevention and better treatment.

Cerebral motor areas along the central fissure provide a different and more sensitive kind of control than the spinal reflexes, the medulla, and the brain stem. In addition, a nearby cortex area provides a muscle sense that keeps you aware of muscle tension and limb movement. This section seems related to other brain areas that are involved (mainly through the skin) with temperature, touch, and pressure. Once again the cortex adds a final bit of control.

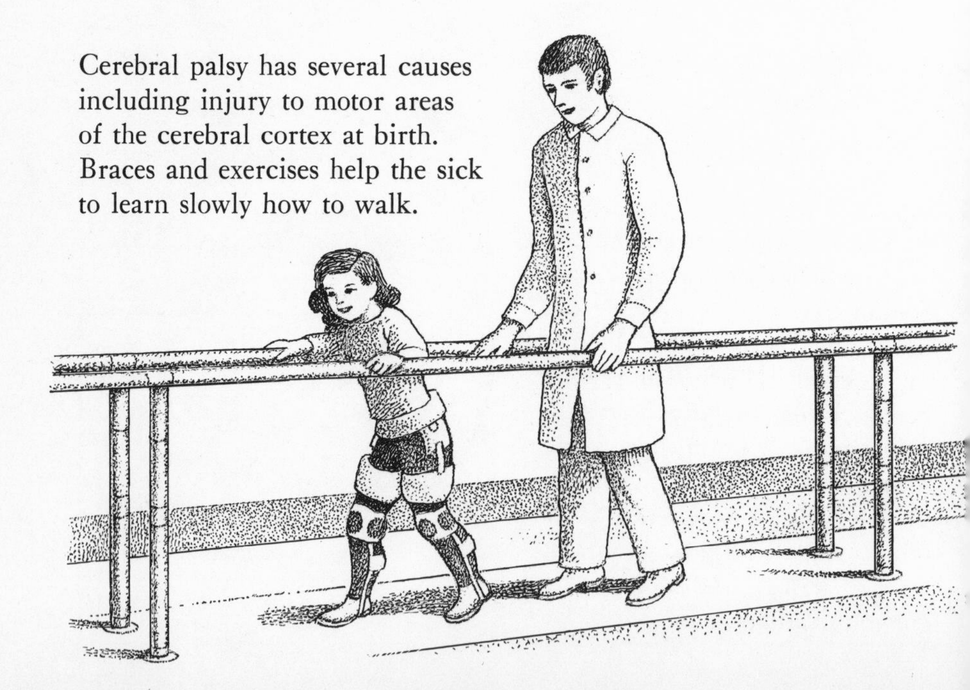

Cerebral palsy has several causes including injury to motor areas of the cerebral cortex at birth. Braces and exercises help the sick to learn slowly how to walk.

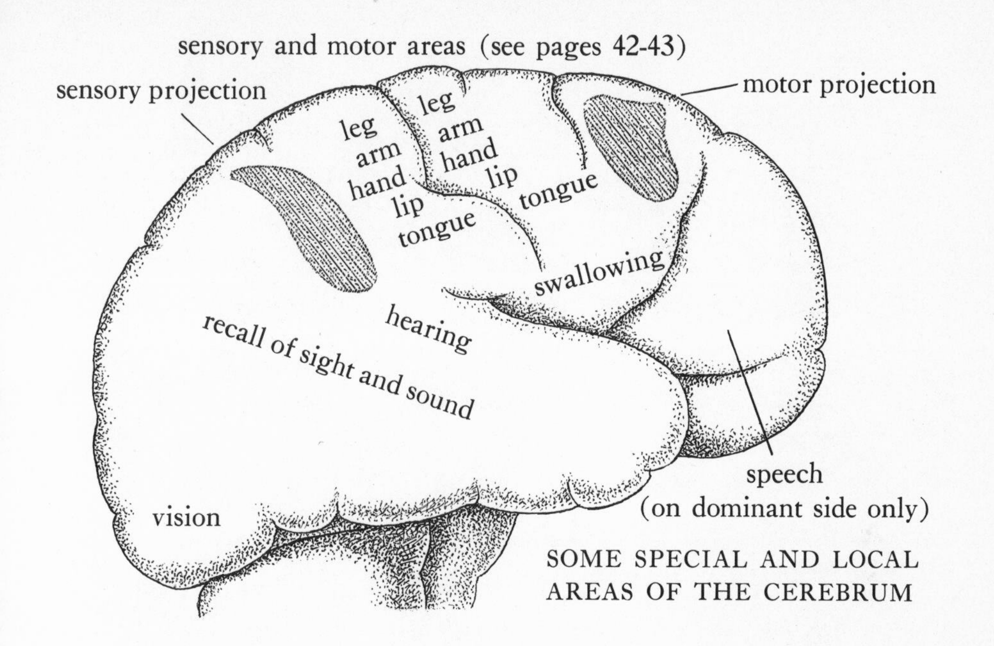

SOME SPECIAL AND LOCAL AREAS OF THE CEREBRUM

Also in the cortex are areas for hearing, which respond to sound stimuli. Similar sensory areas respond to light and receive impulses from the optic nerves that connect to the eye. Small areas responsive to smell and taste have been located too. But much of the cortex remains unidentified, "silent" areas.

Oddly, no part of the cerebrum is sensitive to pain. This feeling is tied to the thalamus in the brain stem. Without the pain sensors, the cerebrum does not feel pain—a boon to the brain surgeon. Neither does the cortex respond directly to signals, such as hunger and thirst, from the body interior.

Stop a minute to see your cerebrum in action.

You come home from school, drop your books on the floor, walk into the kitchen. On the table your mother has a better snack than you really deserve. Your senses tell you immediately what it is. You see a glass of milk and apple pie. Even before you get close, you know from the vapors you see rising that the pie is hot. As you come closer, your sense of smell supports your sense of sight and confirms that fact that hot apple pie is waiting.

At the same time you see all the kitchen, including your mother. Your brain recognizes the familiar things for what they are: table, chairs, stove, refrigerator, and cabinets. These items—your mother and the food you like—add up to a picture that has meaning for you. You know and understand where you are and what to expect.

Your mind goes even further, and you experience feelings about the things you see and recognize. One feeling might be: I am hungry; it is just what I wanted; it's good to be home. But if along the way home you have demolished two hamburgers or three hot dogs, your feeling might be: I can't eat another thing; just the sight of food makes me sick.

You bring new factors and feelings into the situation that depend on you and your condition as well as on the kitchen and its contents. Your reaction may range from satisfaction and joy to disgust or irritation, depending as much on how you feel about your mother and your home as about the kitchen and the food.

By this time motor reactions started by your cerebrum should be well under way. In less time than you take to read this paragraph (if you are hungry), you gulp down the milk, you eat the pie, and you probably call for more.

What you do about a snack or any other matter that demands decision and action is determined by your cerebrum. Your behavior comes partly from specific sensory areas, but more from general areas that make up the bulk of your cerebrum and hence the bulk of your entire brain. These vague areas are the association areas, considered the most highly developed parts of your brain—and the least known.

Much of what you rate as important in life—learning, memory, planning, imagination, reason, intelligence, and even personality—depends on your cerebrum. Using all you have inherited and all you have learned, your cerebrum pictures your world. It starts the specific actions that make you a distinct and special person.

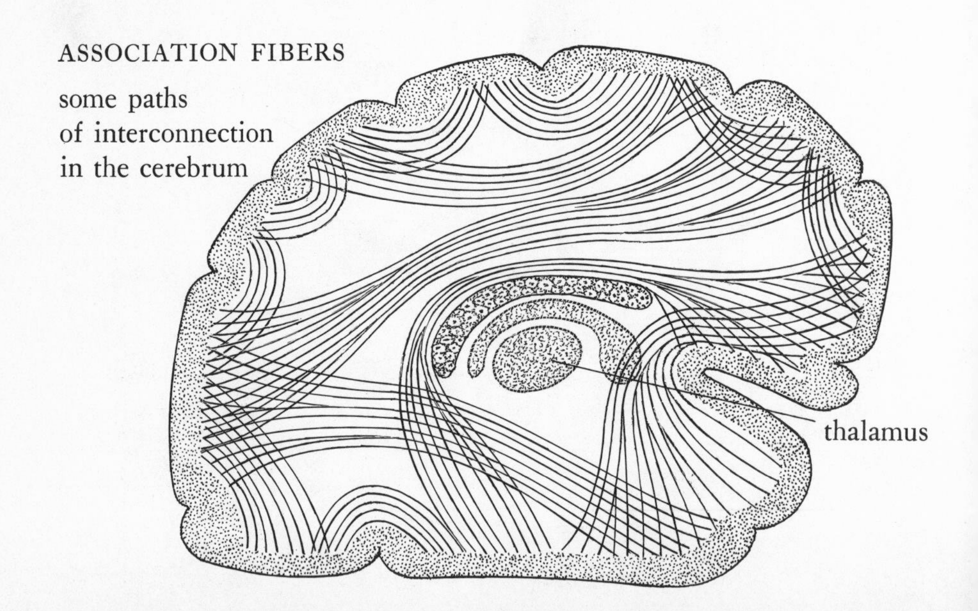

ASSOCIATION FIBERS

some paths of interconnection in the cerebrum

A wavelength of light about 0.00026 inch long will affect every normal human eye in about the same way. But, because of who you are and what you have learned, you interpret this light, when you see it in a special place, as the red light of a traffic signal. What you do depends on information stored in your cerebrum and decisions you make based on that information. You stop. Circumstances are part of the process too. There may be a time when you ignore the red light because of a serious emergency.

At other times red means something else to you besides a traffic light. You can think quickly of many other meanings and ideas that you associate with the single, short word *red*.

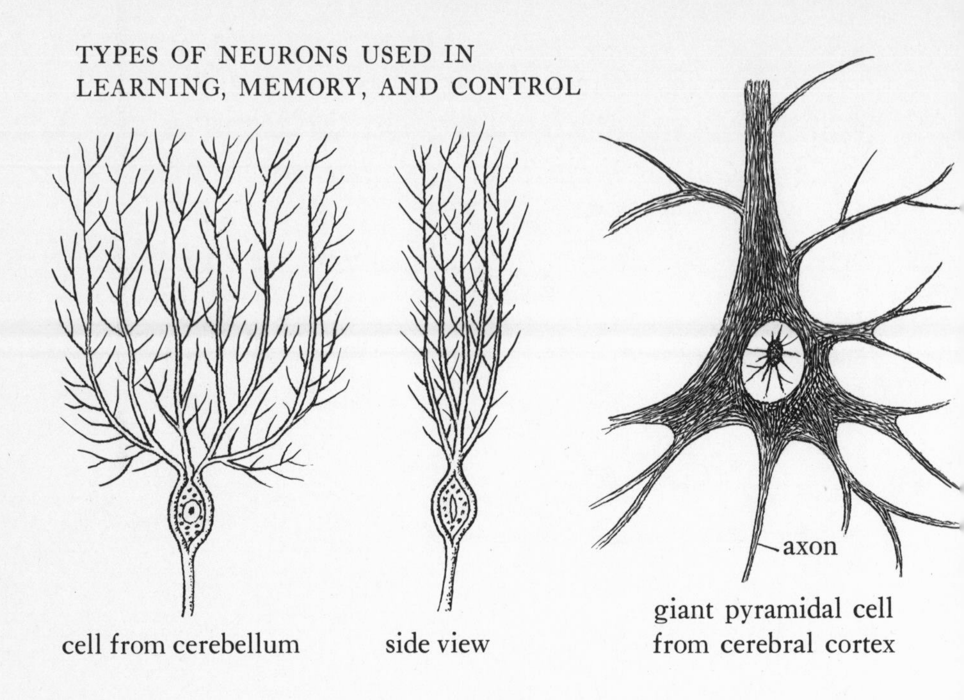

cell from cerebellum

side view

giant pyramidal cell from cerebral cortex

The association areas of your cerebrum work in thousands of ways and involve all kinds of relationships. Studying the nerve cells of these areas gives only scant clues as to how they work. Here the neurons probably form intricate networks, instead of clumps of cells doing the same job. In the association areas, the main task is learning and storing information. If nerve cells of an area are injured or destroyed, the cells are not replaced but another area may relearn the information, and so a function may be restored in whole or in part.

The marvels of memory, recall, and association tempt some people to think that the brain is a supercomputer. Some even have tried to estimate how big a computer would be needed to do the work of an ordinary, average brain. However, no computer can be made to do all that your brain can do. Some things it can do better; others it cannot do at all.

Only parts of the brain, especially the nonthinking parts, work somewhat like computers. Even here there are striking differences. The electrical conductors of a computer are relatively simple, those of the brain, highly complex. Computers work with single input signals, and they can work very rapidly. The brain is not nearly as rapid, but it works with a much wider range of signals. It accepts input from all aspects of the environment.

While computers solve certain mathematical problems rapidly, they do not think. A computer can quickly try all possible responses to a problem till it hits the right one. The human brain applies experience, acts on hunches, and takes shortcuts. While it works more slowly, the brain, with its insight, can get a better answer to some problems. No computer can duplicate yet the billion or more neurons of your cerebrum.

Some of your brain works like no computer yet made. Other parts, like the cerebellum, seem to follow the pattern of a digital computer, still others that of an analog computer.

The brain's control of the body uses an analog kind of action. For example, as a day gets hotter, the liquid in a thermometer rises. Its changing height shows the change in temperature.

As the day gets hotter, new sensory messages go to your brain. As the thermometer climbs, your brain takes action to prevent damage by overheating. You begin to perspire; your thirst increases; more blood flows through your skin. These and other actions help cool your body. They slow up or stop as the temperature goes down.

The brain, especially its overdeveloped cerebrum, acts like an organized system that is equipped to maintain and improve itself. It detects, communicates, sorts, and distributes signals. With this stimulation, it issues new signals, activating muscles and glands. It does this work in general learned patterns that are modified to meet specific situations. Through speech and writing, brains affect one another. Not only do individuals act and survive, the community survives also.

The cerebrum and its association areas are the parts of your brain for which you may use the word *mind*. What we call mind is certainly related to the brain, but it is not a specific part that can be located clearly.

The very way we use the word *mind* suggests that it has more than a single meaning. We say "mind the baby," but we also say "mind your mother," and "improve your mind." Another idea is involved when we say "keep it in mind," or "never mind," phrases that imply remembering and forgetting.

The unabridged dictionaries show how difficult it is to define mind. One dictionary has 44 uses for the word; another has 24, not counting subuses. Mind stresses consciousness, the ability to perceive something, within or without. The mind is the part of the brain that wills, thinks, feels, reasons, perceives, and judges. All these activities involve the cerebrum.

Understanding the mind may be more difficult than understanding the brain. How do you decide which book to read?

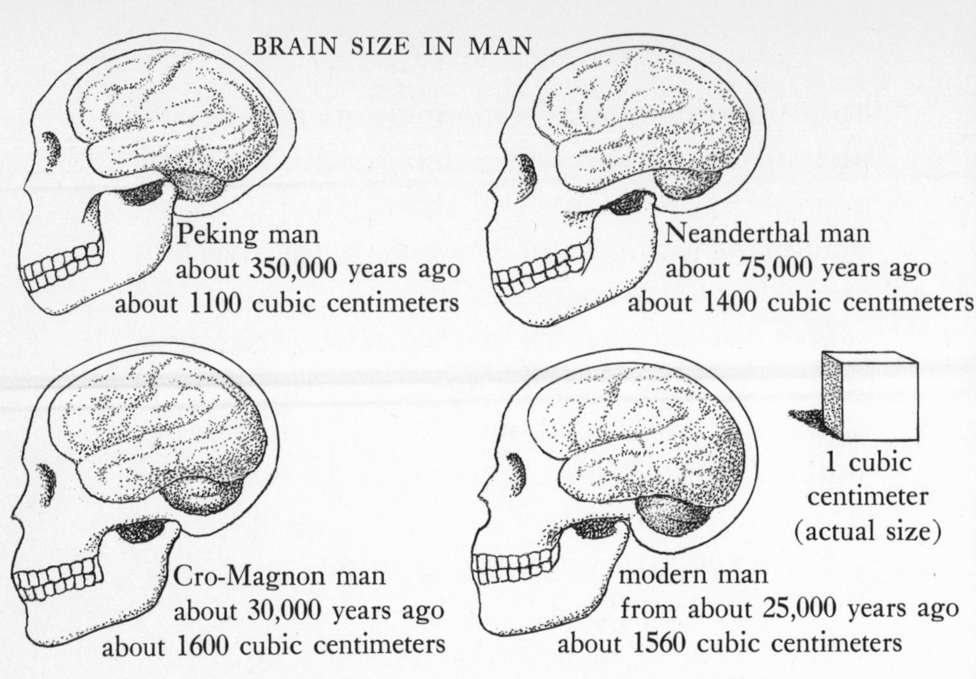

Brain size has not changed much the past 5000 years, but the human mind has changed greatly.

While your brain and mind are not the same thing, your mind dwells in your cerebrum because all the things you have learned are stored there. All that you have learned and remembered, and even a good deal of what you think you have forgotten, contribute to your mind. In short, your mind is your whole outlook on the world, as you know it through your central nervous system. Nothing that you can name or mention can be excluded from your mind. Your mind is growing and changing all the time. It includes not only your intelligence, but much more.

Diseases or injuries can hurt the mind, so it may become limited or distorted. Disease can affect the mind and a person's behavior without producing any change in the brain. Mental health and mental disease are difficult fields in which doctors are making progress slowly.

DISEASES OF THE BRAIN AND MIND

These fall into two groups: *Organic diseases* show an injury or change in the brain or nerves that is related to the disease. Examples: Polio, nerves destroyed by a virus; multiple sclerosis, scar tissue forms; cerebral palsy causes organic damage to the brain. *Functional diseases* show no changes in the cells, or tissues of the brain and nervous system, as in neuroses and psychoses.

Neuroses are mental diseases in which a person is not withdrawn from reality nor is violent. He can cope with life, but he may be anxious, angry, disturbed, or depressed. These conditions may begin in childhood. Examples: Phobias or exaggerated fears, as fear of thunder or of airplanes. Compulsions (doing things without need in patterned ways), as washing hands dozens of times a day. People with neuroses are often anxious and disturbed about things that normal people accept. Psychoses are severe functional disorders in which people withdraw from the real world or give strange meanings to daily happenings. Example: Schizophrenia is a withdrawal into a world of fantasy. Perhaps someone feels that he is a great person or has great power. Paranoia is an intense feeling that people are against you and are persecuting you.

These two groups of mental diseases are usually functional, but sometimes they are organic. There are also groups of illnesses that seem to have a mental or emotional cause, but affect physical organs. Examples: Asthma, ulcers, and migraine headaches.

Another complication is that the mind of an Eskimo, a Zulu, or an Apache Indian may be different from yours in some ways, because of the different ways each of you has lived. Even small variations within the same home may produce important mental contrasts among children. Age, sex, schooling, work, race, and nationality all have an influence on your mind. Each mind in the world is special. There is no one exactly like you, and no mind that is the exact duplicate of yours.

Different life patterns produce different mental patterns and ways of looking at life and at the world.

TEST YOUR MEMORY

Get a clock or watch with a second hand, some paper and a pencil, and someone to time you. Read these instructions carefully: twice if you wish.

In the picture on page 34 people are doing different things. Some may be doing more than one thing at a time. After you have gone over these directions, have the person with the watch time you for ten seconds. Study the picture. At the end of that time, shut the book and write the answers to these two questions:

1. How many men and how many women are in the picture?
2. What is each of them doing?

Score one point for each fact you remember correctly. Do not peek in advance. Now when your partner says "go," turn to page 34 and begin.

Behind this concept of the mind are ideas that are important but hard to explain. Memory is one of them, for without memory, intelligence is impossible. Your memory includes all kinds of things that seem to be forgotten in a moment, but it also includes others that are just as clear many years later as they were when they happened.

Decision making is another cerebral task. Just how does a person decide what to do? Judgment and creativity, too, are further aspects of the mind. Perhaps more important than any one ability is the organizing and pulling together of all the sensations, ideas, and memories you have into patterns that make for a happy, useful life.

What you know, what you remember, and what you are modify the sensations you get through your eyes, ears, nose, and mouth. These sensations are mixed, sorted, and stored by the silent areas of your cerebrum. Memories may be the actual facts you recall. More often they include also the feelings that have developed around some past action. Emotions are usually a part of anything you do, or of any thought or memory.

It may be only dull to remember 12 times 12 equals 144. But Henry may recall at the same time how hard it was for him to learn multiplication, and how he did those dull problems over and over again. He may remember punishments like staying after school. So Henry prefers to remember fun and happy times. Both kinds of feelings color his life and help the boy decide what he wants to do.

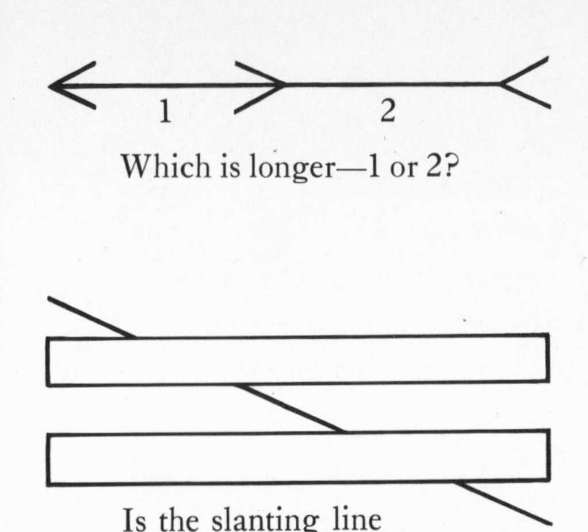

Which is longer—1 or 2?

Is the slanting line straight or broken?

The way your mind "sees" the world is a result of long training. For example, you know that a truck, far away, which looks no larger than your hand, is really 30 feet long. Even though the truck looks small, you know it is big. But at other times our eyes fool us as in these four pictures. Your eyes are tricked by the surroundings to give you the wrong view or perception. Check the 3 pictures at left with a ruler.

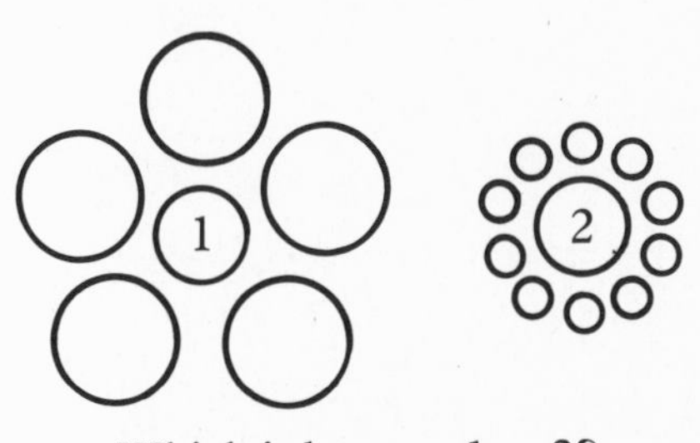

Which is larger—1 or 2?

Which do you see—two black faces or one white vase?

In general, what you call your mind gives you an overall picture of the world. Through your mind you perceive sights and sounds in a special way. Facts, associations, and memories, all colored by feelings, become part of your mind and its intelligence. You use them to make decisions, solve problems, and live your own life.

The realm of the mind is not the same as the brain, though both are closely connected. The brain is a physical thing that can be weighed, measured, mapped, and described. Experiments with rats and monkeys and even with people help disclose the working of the brain. It detects and protects. It molds your body into a smooth machine.

Your mind does more than this. It is an outgrowth of your brain, not a part of it. It is a part of you, but it is also a part of your family, friends, and community. Only a few less important parts of the mind can be measured, and these only in a gross way. The measure of intelligence, for example, is beset with difficulties. So the mind is real and unreal at the same time. If the mind of a baby is not nurtured with love and stimulation, its growth is impaired just as though the infant did not receive enough food.

Brain waves give a clue to some of the ways the brain works.

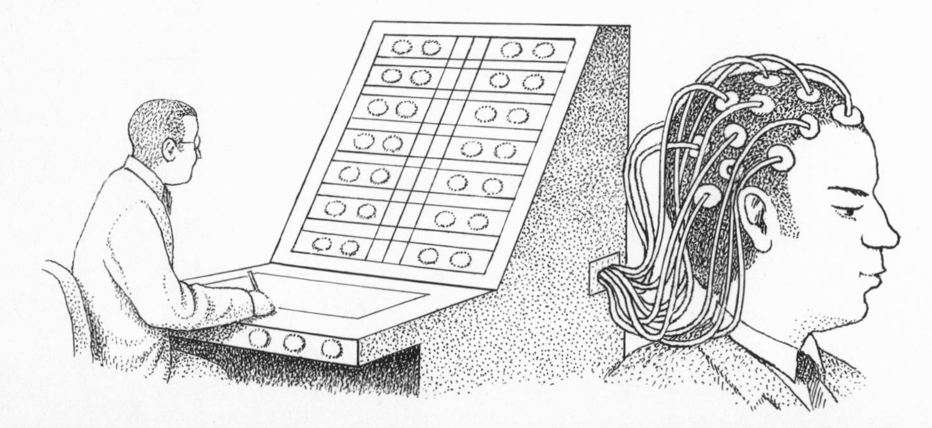

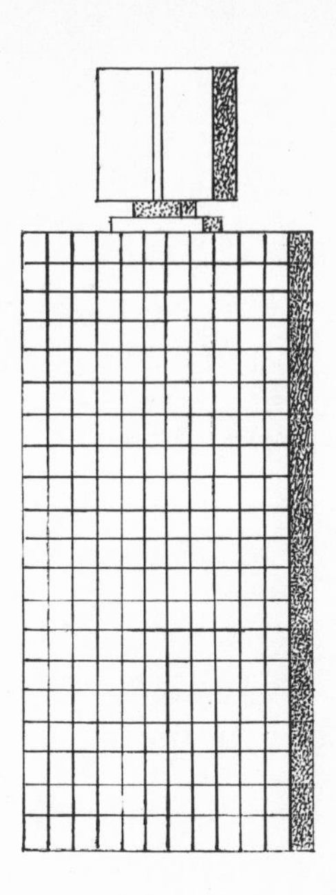

In an experiment, monkeys were taken from their mother when very young and given an artificial mother. The babies clearly preferred the soft, cloth-covered artificial mother to cling to even though the wire artificial mother was built to give them food.

Warmth, softness, and affection help young animals to grow and are needed as much as food and drink.

To know the brain, you also must know the mind. Your mind is what is absorbing, sorting, appraising, and storing away the meaning of the small black symbols that stretch across these pages line after line. But the two work as a unit. Your brain was a billion years in the making, but your mind is much younger.

From that long past your brain has become the most complex, delicate, and powerful organ of your body. We still know very little about the brain. Don't abuse it with alcohol or other drugs. Your brain and mind shape the most important thing in the world—that special and unique being called *you*.

INDEX

** Indicates illustrations*